THE AGGRETSUKO
GUIDE TO OFFICE LIFE

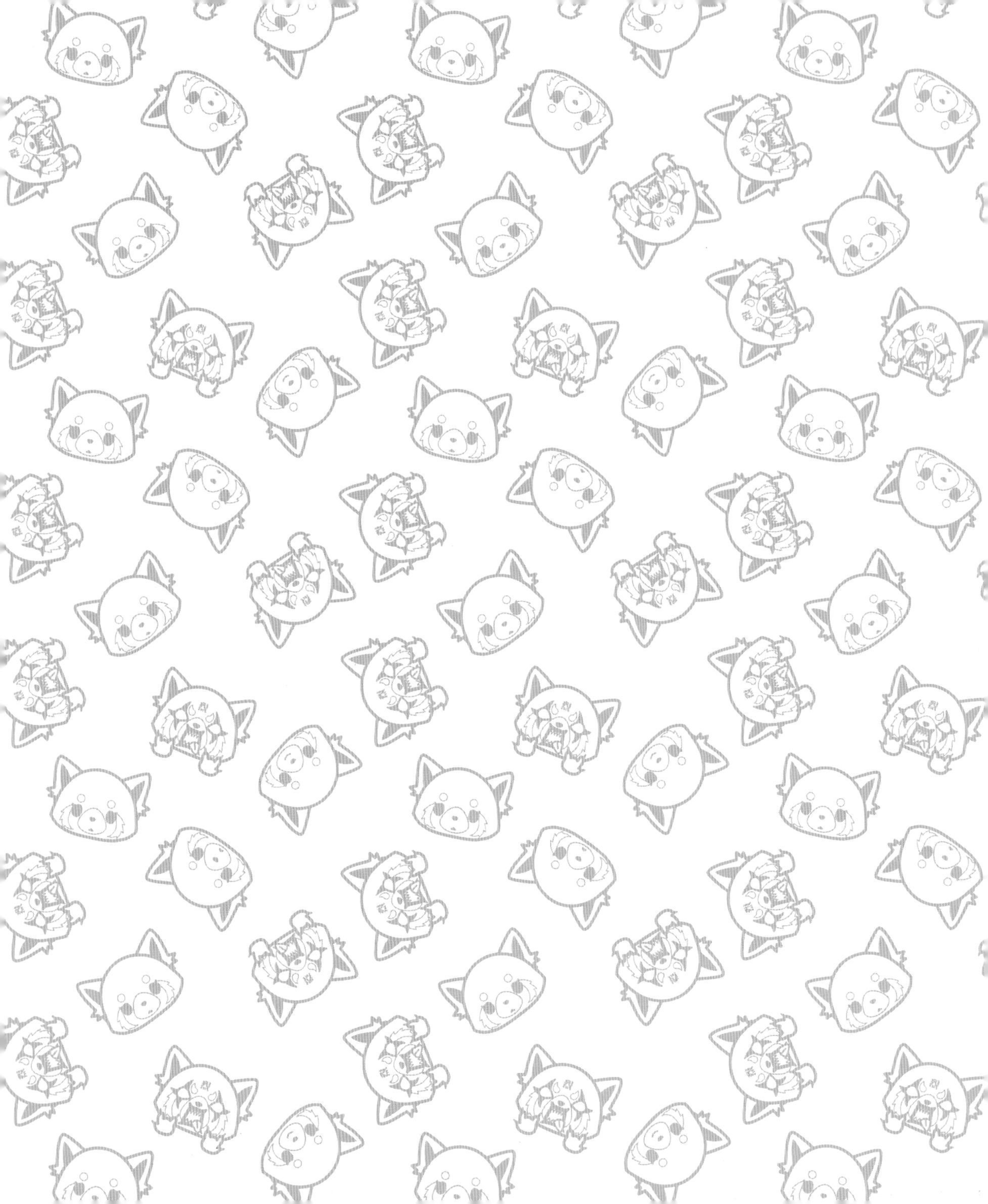

THE Aggretsuko™
GUIDE TO OFFICE LIFE

CHRONICLE BOOKS
SAN FRANCISCO

CHRONICLE BOOKS
680 SECOND STREET
SAN FRANCISCO, CA 94107
WWW.CHRONICLEBOOKS.COM

Library of Congress Cataloging-in-Publication Data available.
ISBN 978-1-4521-7152-4

MIX
Paper from responsible sources
FSC™ C104723
www.fsc.org

Manufactured in China.
Design by Kelly Abeln

Chronicle Books LLC
680 Second Street
San Francisco, CA 94107

www.chroniclebooks.com

10 9 8 7 6 5 4 3 2 1

CONTENTS:

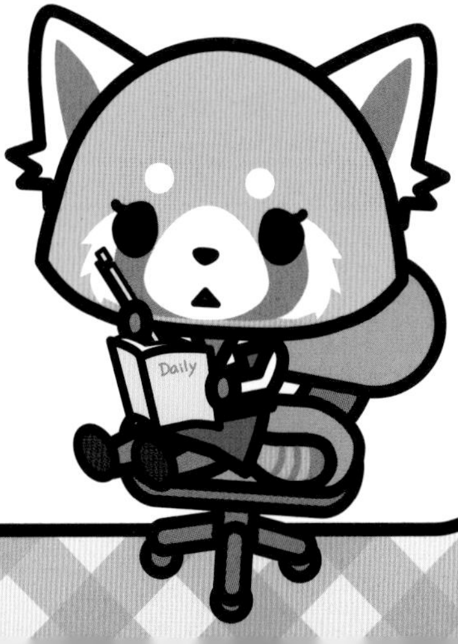
Daily

INTRODUCTION:
Gotta be ready for tomorrow, too!

"What a beautiful day . . .
never mind."

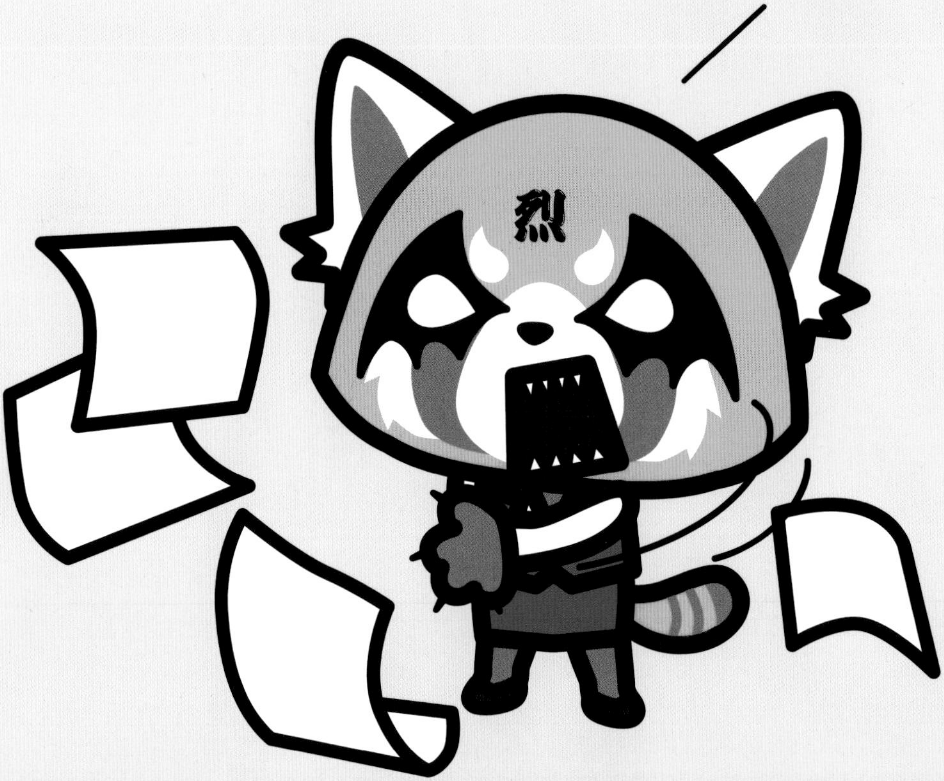
烈

down, my blinders on, and do what I do best: work, work, work, work, and work. Sure, it can be frustrating: like when my boss saunters over to my desk at 5 PM to drop a ton of last-minute billing for me to reconcile, I may have the urge to chainsaw and light the file folders on file.

Look: I'd be lying if I didn't confess that, beneath it all—my cute exterior, my reputation as a hard worker—seethes an inner rage so intense, so all-consuming and aggressive, that I literally transform from a sweet-looking red panda to a beer-guzzling, chicken-wing–eating, karaoke-singing metalhead. I reserve the right to rage every once in a while, and you should, too. But I manage to keep my rage under wraps . . . most of the time.

So, while I dream of one day getting a promotion or telling my well-intentioned though thoroughly annoying colleagues to buzz off, I stave off my pent-up anger by following a steady diet of hardcore heavy metal, Happy Hour and all-you-can-eat specials, and chilling with my friends—though not necessarily in that order—and then bravely carrying on.

This is my guidebook on how to handle everything from the professional doldrums and your colleagues' tantrums to managing every type of corporate personality to navigating mandatory company picnics while staying happy inside. Don't let work get you down. And if it does, it's okay to rage.

Like I always say, tomorrow is a new day!

Hello. My name is Retsuko.

I'm twenty-five years old, a Scorpio, and my blood type is A. Each day I commute thirty minutes in a cramped subway to my job in the accounting department of a respectable trading company. It's always been a dream of mine to work in this field. Unfortunately, I have lots of work, harsh deadlines, and largely unsympathetic bosses. But I keep my head

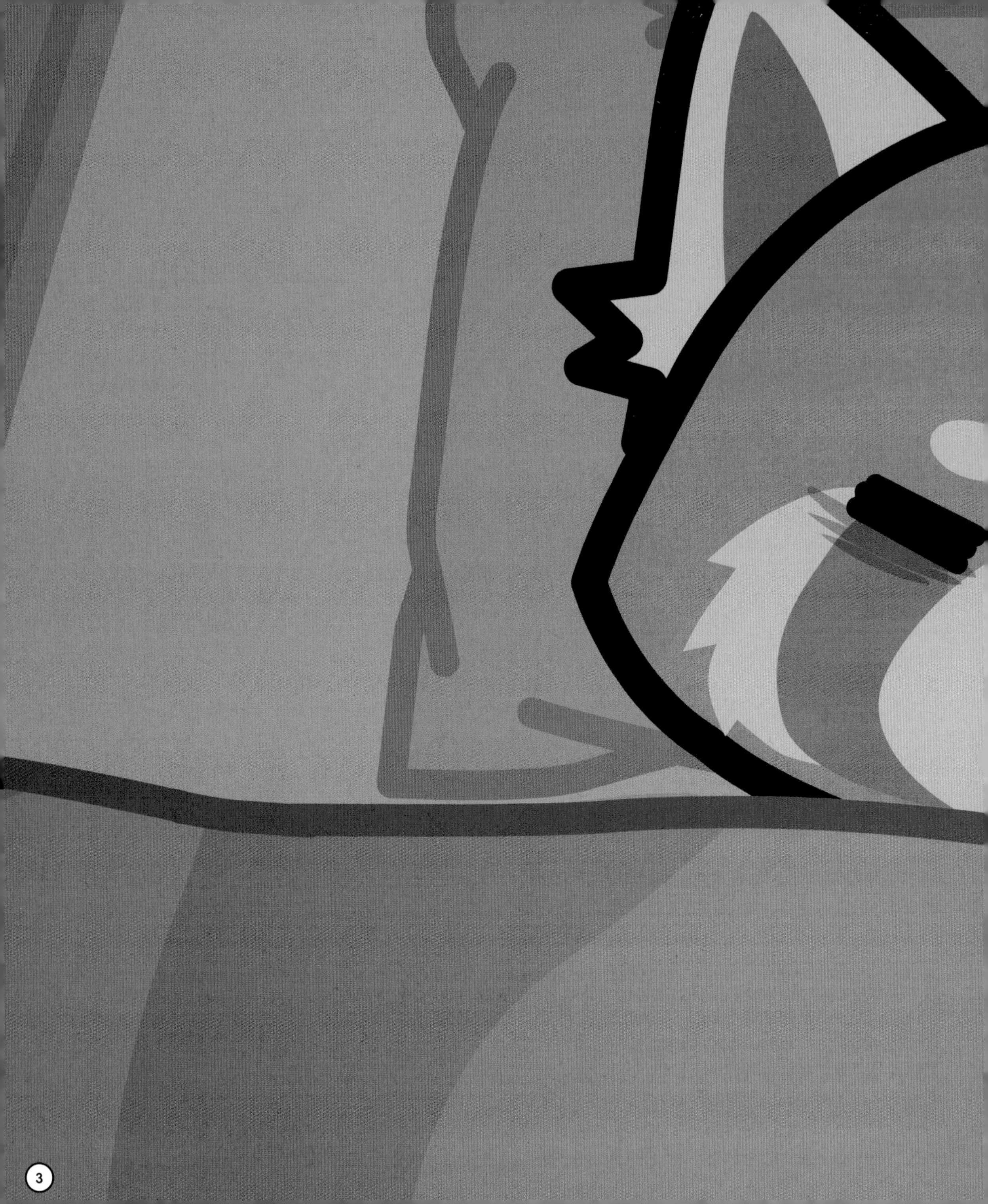

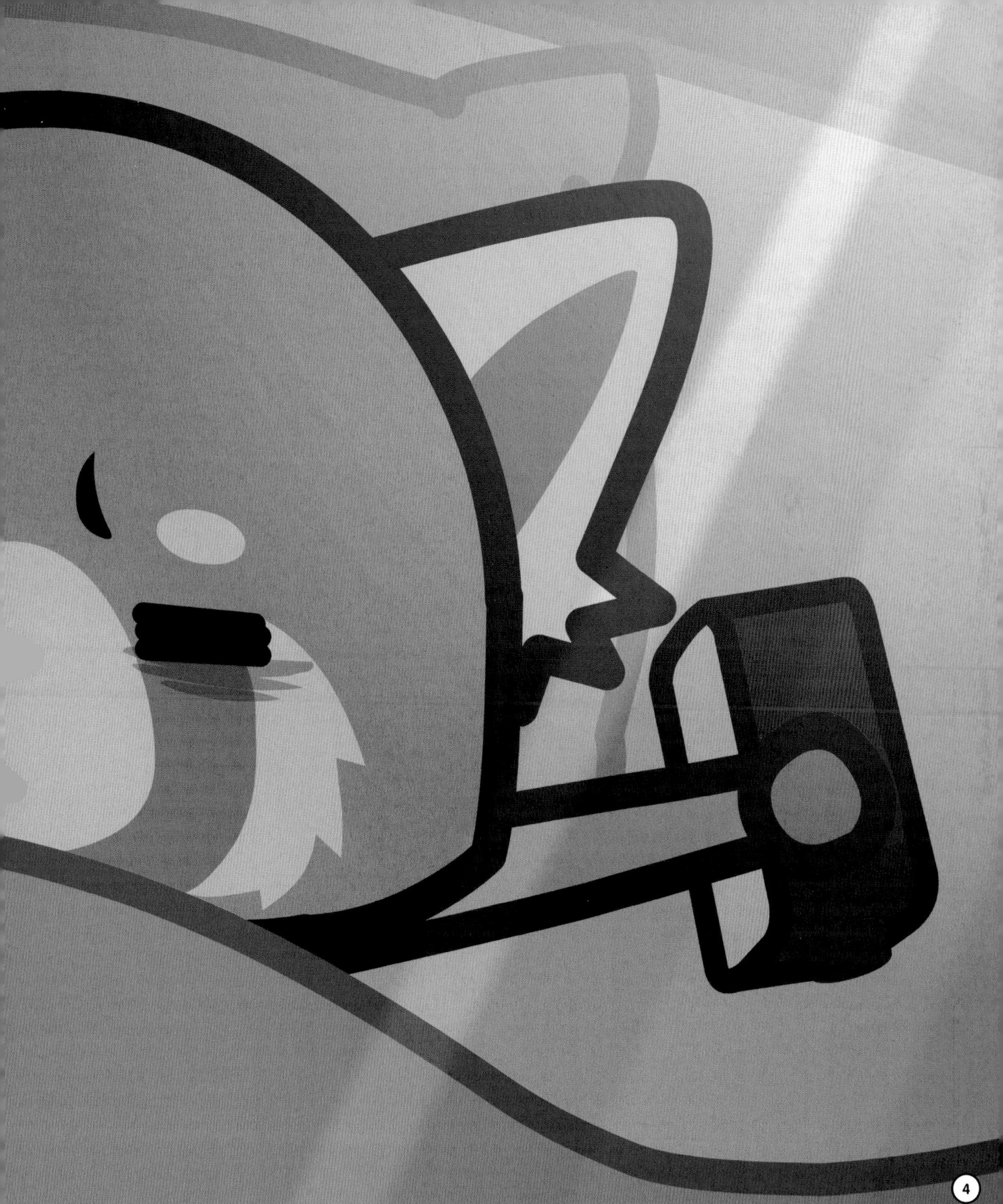

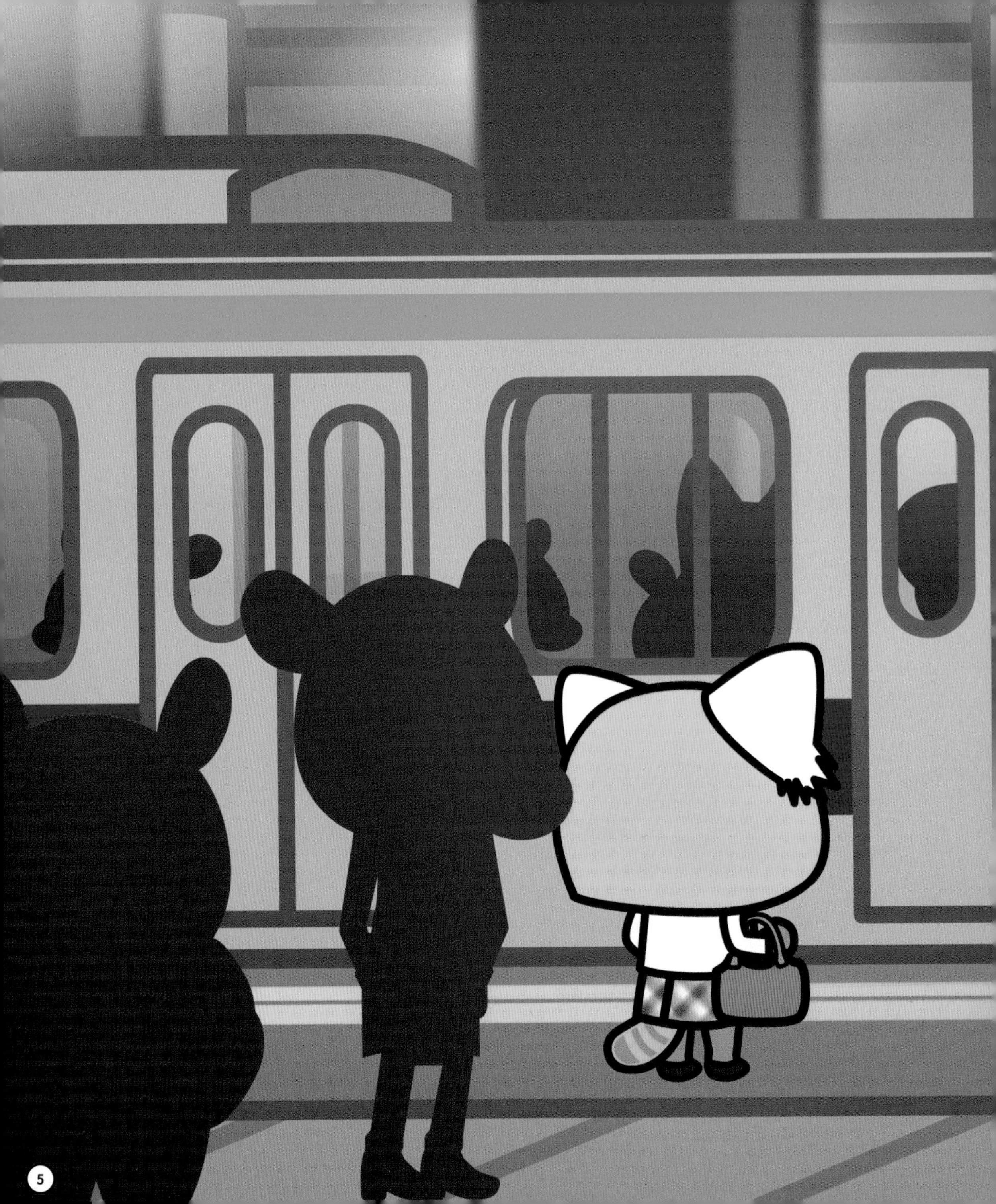

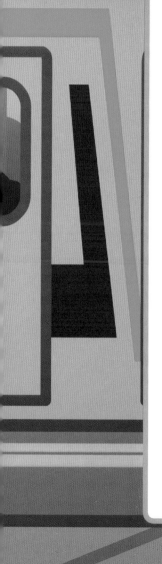

CHAPTER ONE: HIGHWAY TO HELL

Sometimes the hardest part about work is getting there, whether you're stuck in daily bumper-to-bumper traffic, taking a 5 AM bus, or trudging through slushy snow. My morning commute is a thirty minute, cramped subway ride—and that's on a good day. Here's what an average week of commuting looks like:

MONDAY: Commute-snarling track fire. Delayed twenty minutes.

TUESDAY: Tunnel clogged by horde of rats. Train re-routed with no warning. Delayed by fifteen minutes and had to pay an extra fare.

WEDNESDAY: A good travel day minus being dripped on by mysterious brown fluid leaking from train ceiling.

THURSDAY: Train overcrowded by a group of crying toddlers going on a field trip. Delayed by thirty minutes. Did I mention they were *crying*? All twenty of them?

FRIDAY: Dropped my cell phone on train tracks.

The daily commute is just a *part* of your work life, a mere fraction if we're counting it. The moment you step into the office, it's Game On, and don't let anyone tell you any different. You endured track fires, train delays, and an entire army of screaming five-year-olds and you still survived. Now that you made it to work, it's time to shine.

COMMUTING TIP

My alarm clock sets the tone for the rest of my day, and if I haven't already hit the snooze button, I could just as easily smash the clock against the wall. There's nothing like a steadily annoying beeping sound to remind you that you're just a little cog in a very big machine.

Wake up as early as you can so that you can have a few minutes at home to breathe deeply and prepare yourself for what will most likely be a horribly unpleasant journey that you have no choice but to embark upon. Every day. For the rest of your adult life. Embrace some quiet time at home while you can. Deep breaths!

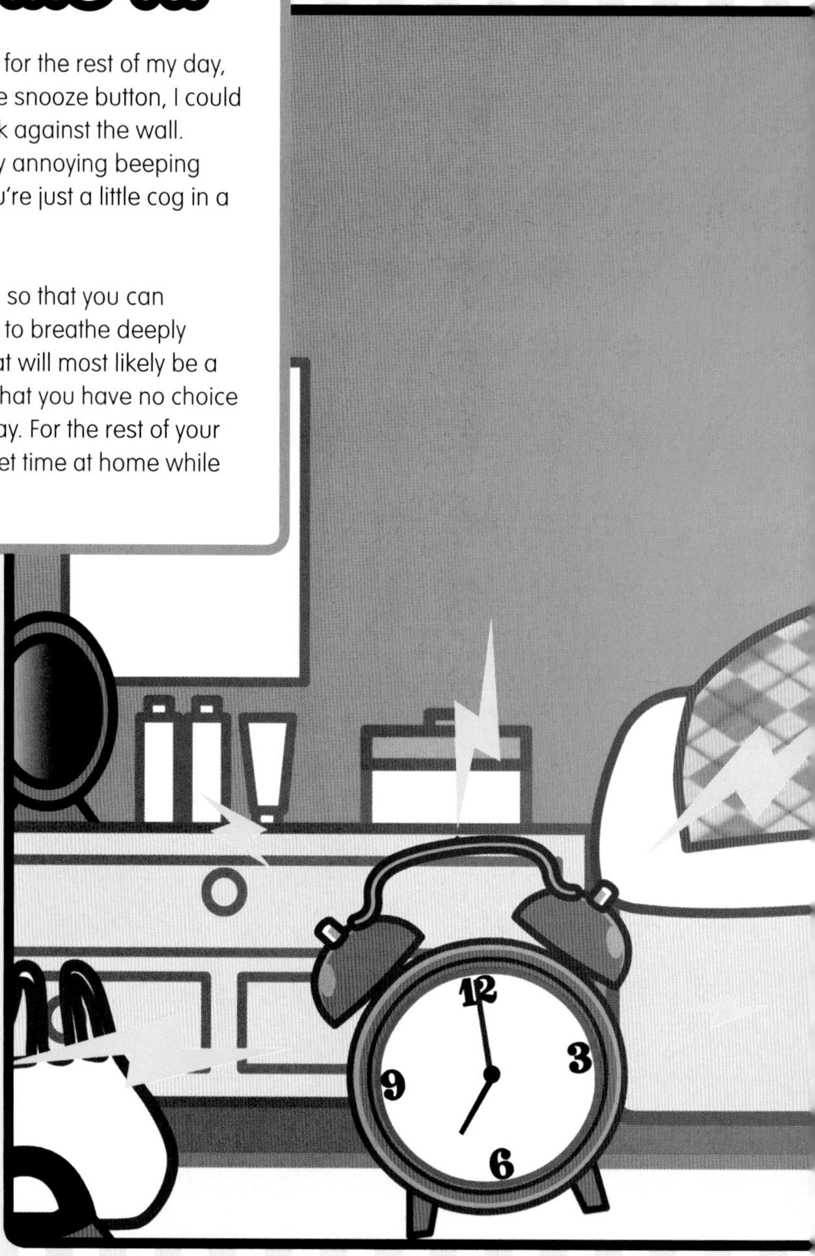

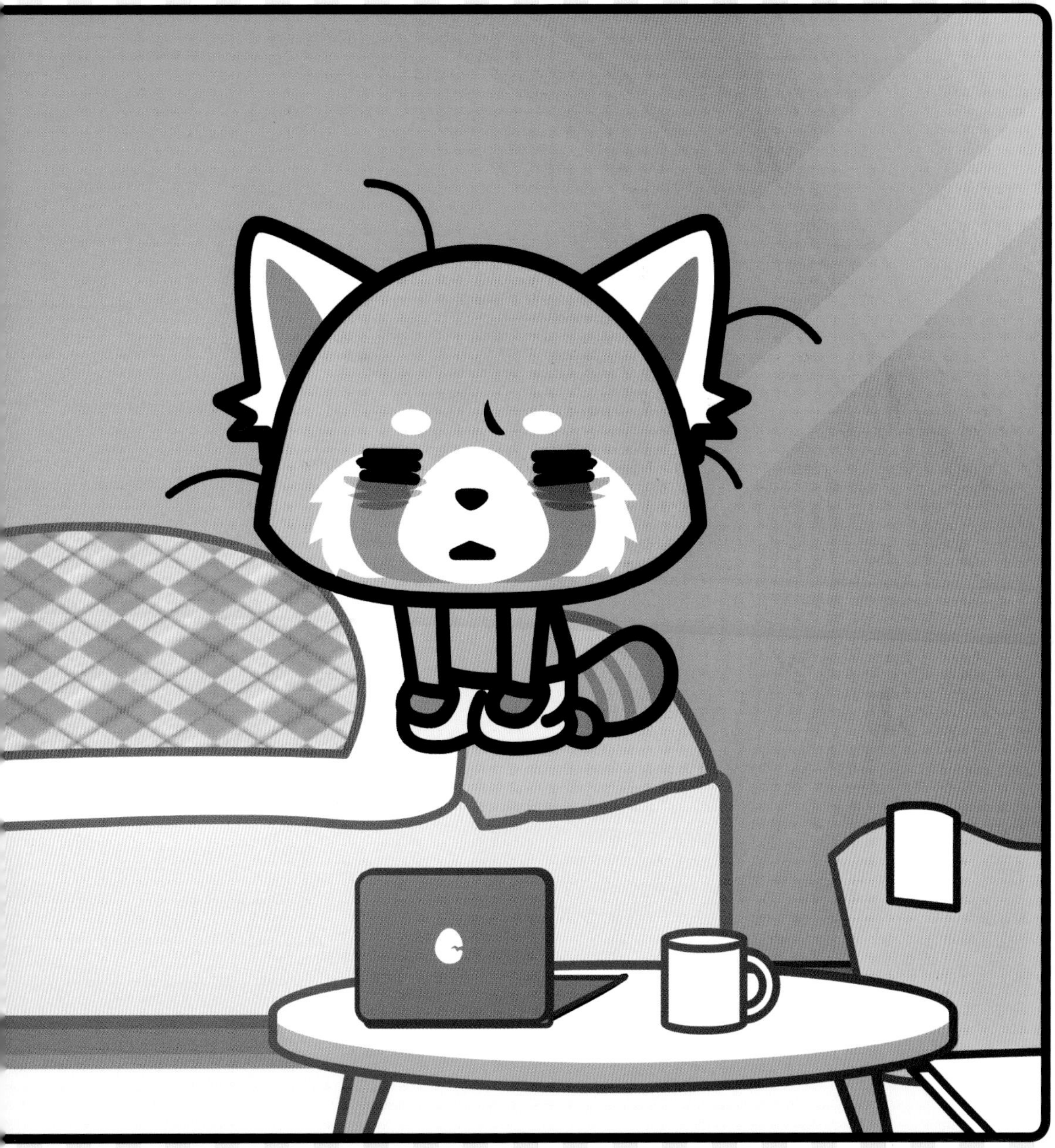

SUBWAY ETIQUETTE

Here are my top tips for basic etiquette while riding the subway:

1. The pregnant woman—you know, the bearer of life—gets the empty seat, not your backpack full of dirty gym socks and half-eaten bag of chips.

2. A word of warning: the mysteriously empty subway car is usually empty for a reason.

3. Eating takeout—fermented pork in onion relish and garlic tofu—is one way to clear out a car. Or you could be a normal and nice, thoughtful individual, and save the stinky food for home.

4. Avoid eye contact unless it's an emergency or you happen to see that cute bearded guy with the bike messenger's bag. Then, by all means, bat away.

5. Don't break out the break-dancing unless you actually know what you're doing. While we're on the subject, no one wants to hear the song you're jamming to.

6. Three words: No. More. Manspreading.

7. Take off your backpack so that you don't smack people in the face with it, and so that you don't take up more room than necessary.

8. Let people who are getting off the train out before you get on. I mean, come on.

9. Try to avoid reading over your fellow commuters' shoulders—or their texts!

10. This isn't your personal bathroom: don't clip your fingernails here.

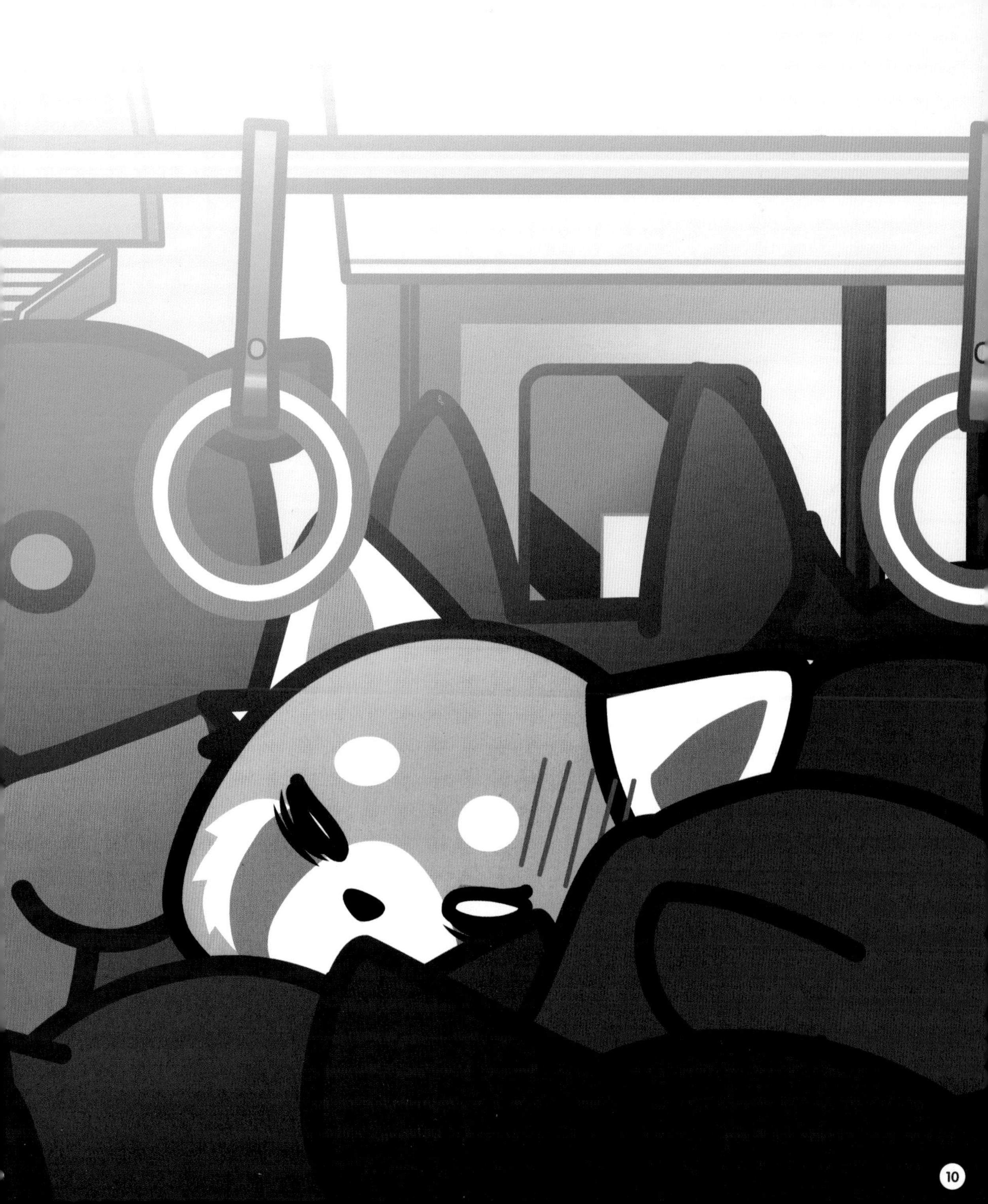

THE BOSS

At least at one point in your (unfortunate) work life, you'll encounter a boss like mine. Besides his horrible time-management skills, my boss has zero problem cruising out of work early and bullying his employees (ahem, me) for not picking up the slack whenever he falls short. As if that weren't enough, the man delivers bad puns and even worse jokes.

You can handle the bosses of the world in one of two ways: (1) laugh along with him (and feel a part of you die inside) or (2) rage. I'm pretty sure your job description doesn't include "killing yourself slowly with forced acceptance of bad puns" or "executive-level work" at "non-executive pay level" and, if it does, you need a different game book altogether. Take a page outta my book instead, and embrace your inner aggro-metalhead. The next time your boss has you cornered by the water cooler to practice his comedy routine, go to your happy place and imagine yourself doing the most awesome stage dive while screaming obscenities at him.

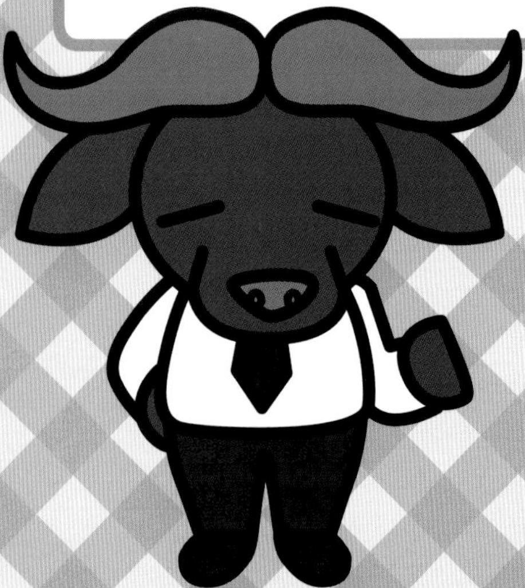

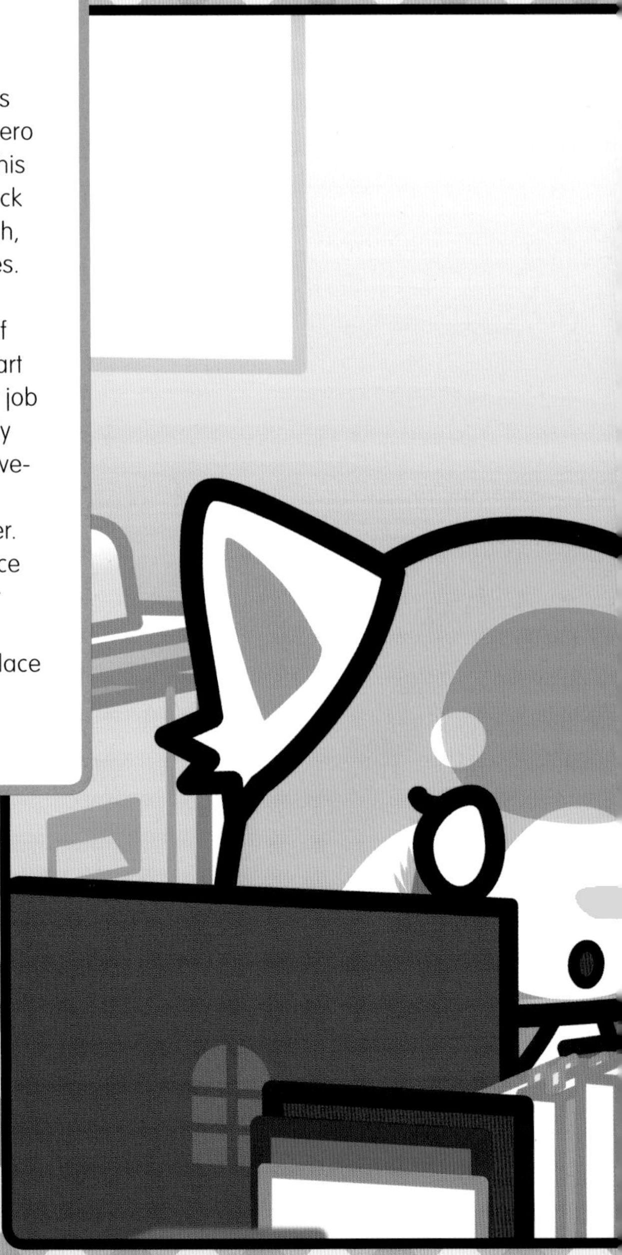

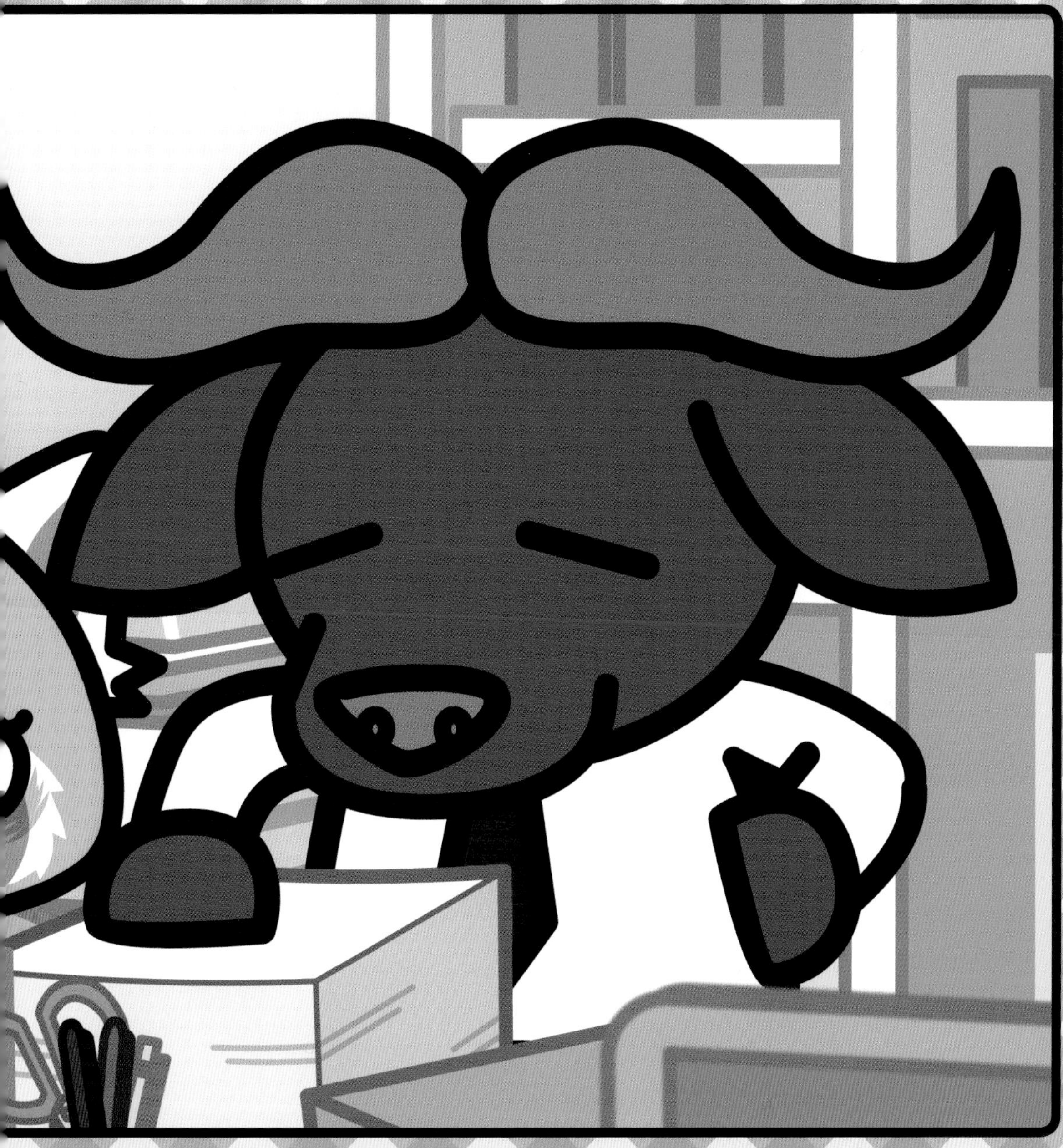

ELEVATOR CHALLENGE

Here's a fun game: run like a gazelle to see if your co-worker manages to not close the elevator door on your head for the umpteenth time.

* **HINT:** You will always lose this game. Even if you make it in, now you have to spend that awkward time in the elevator next to someone who didn't hold the door for you.

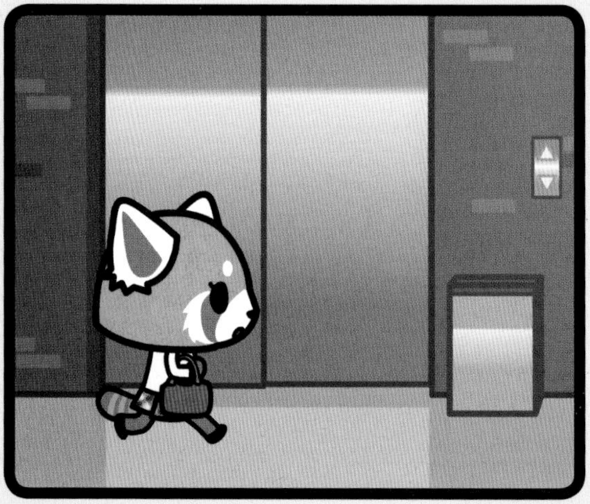

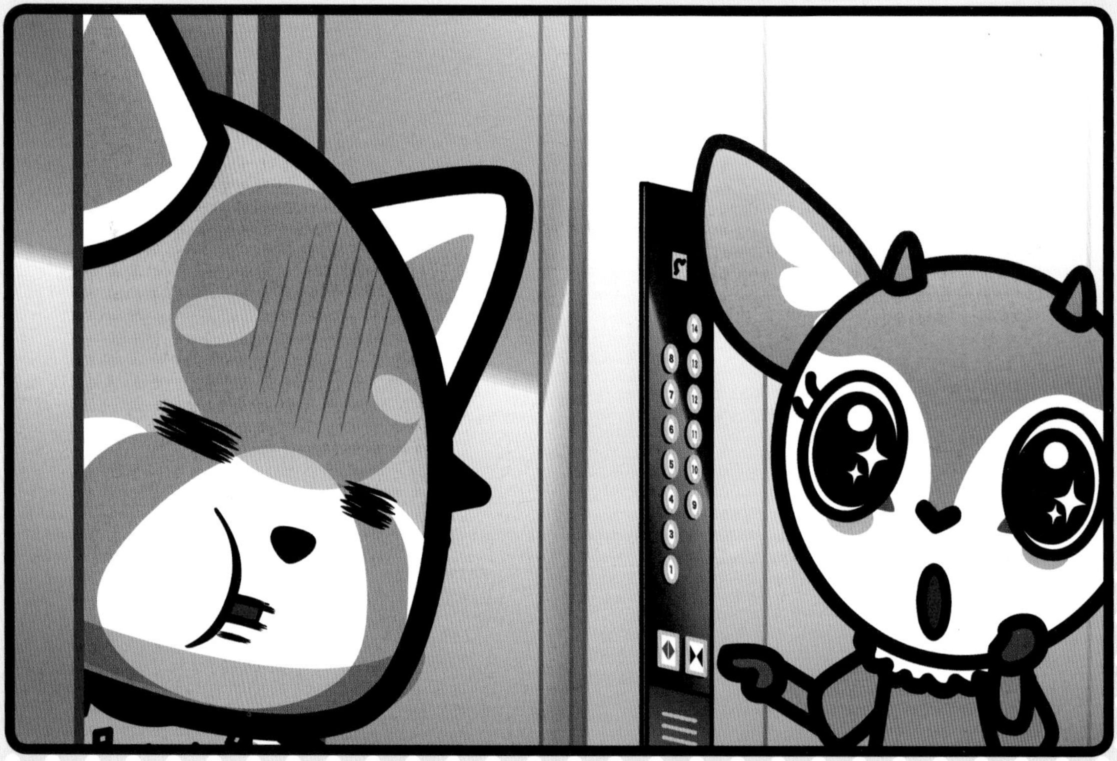

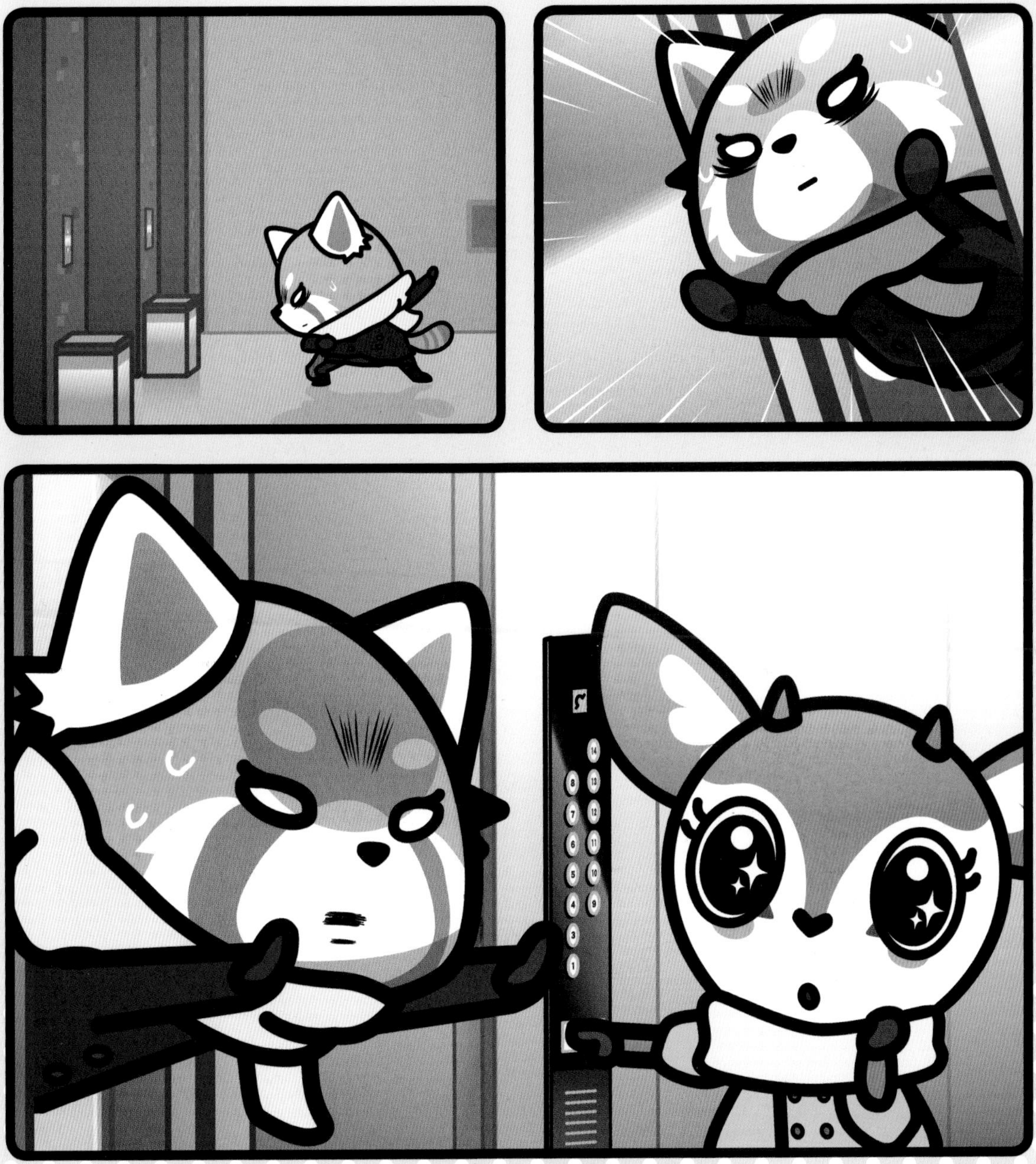

TIP

For some free entertainment, position yourself behind someone who's sending rapid fire text messages and watch the drama unfold.

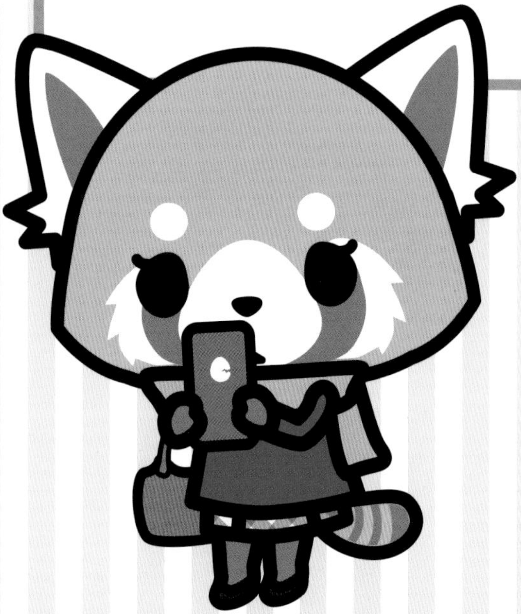

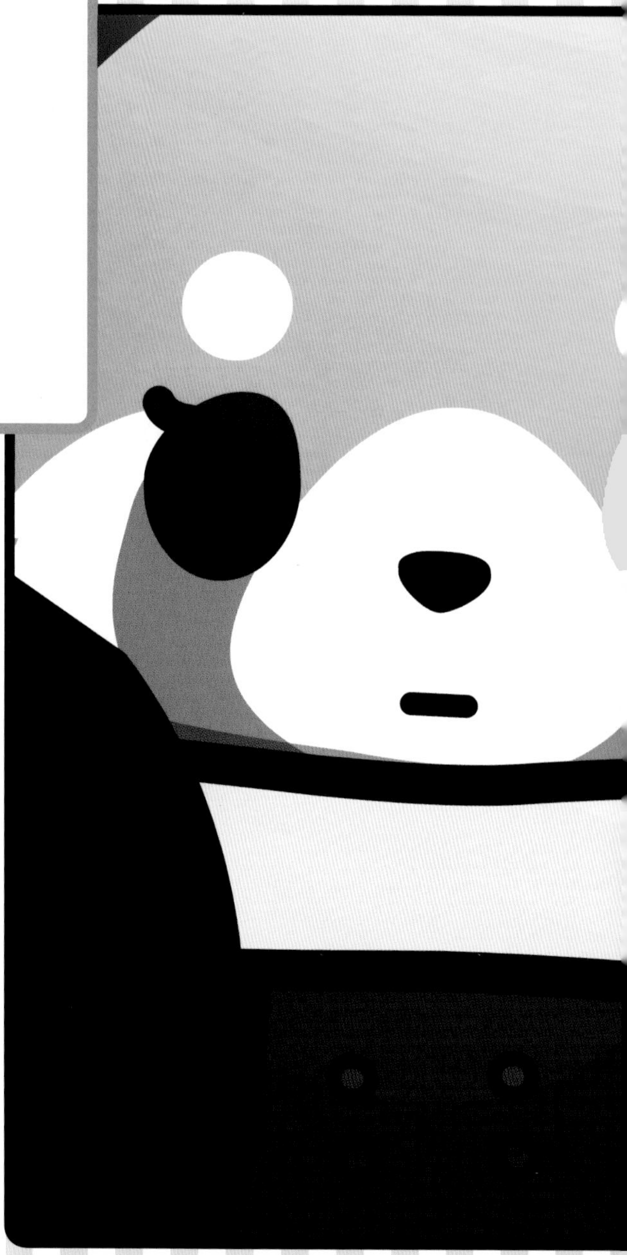

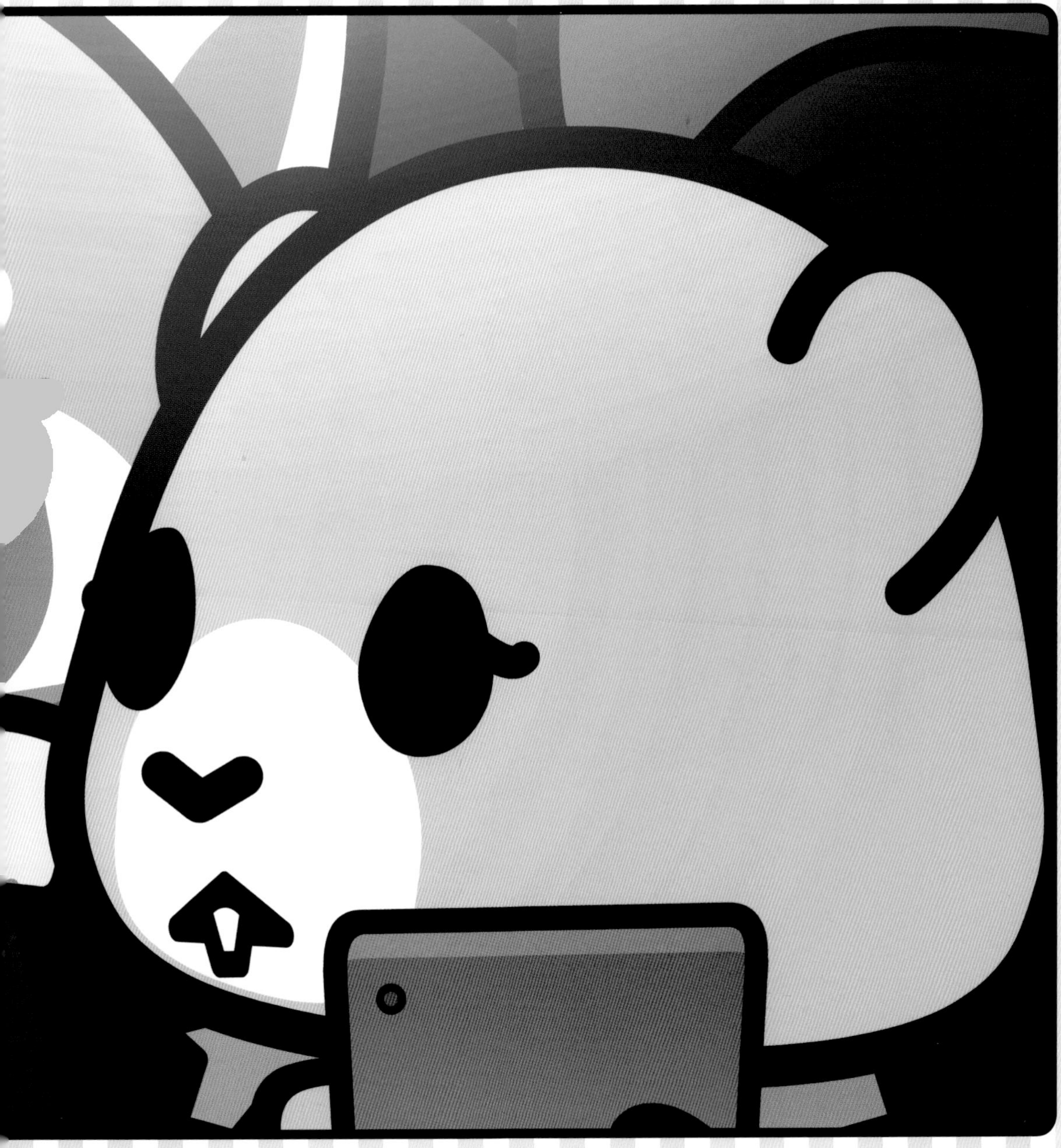

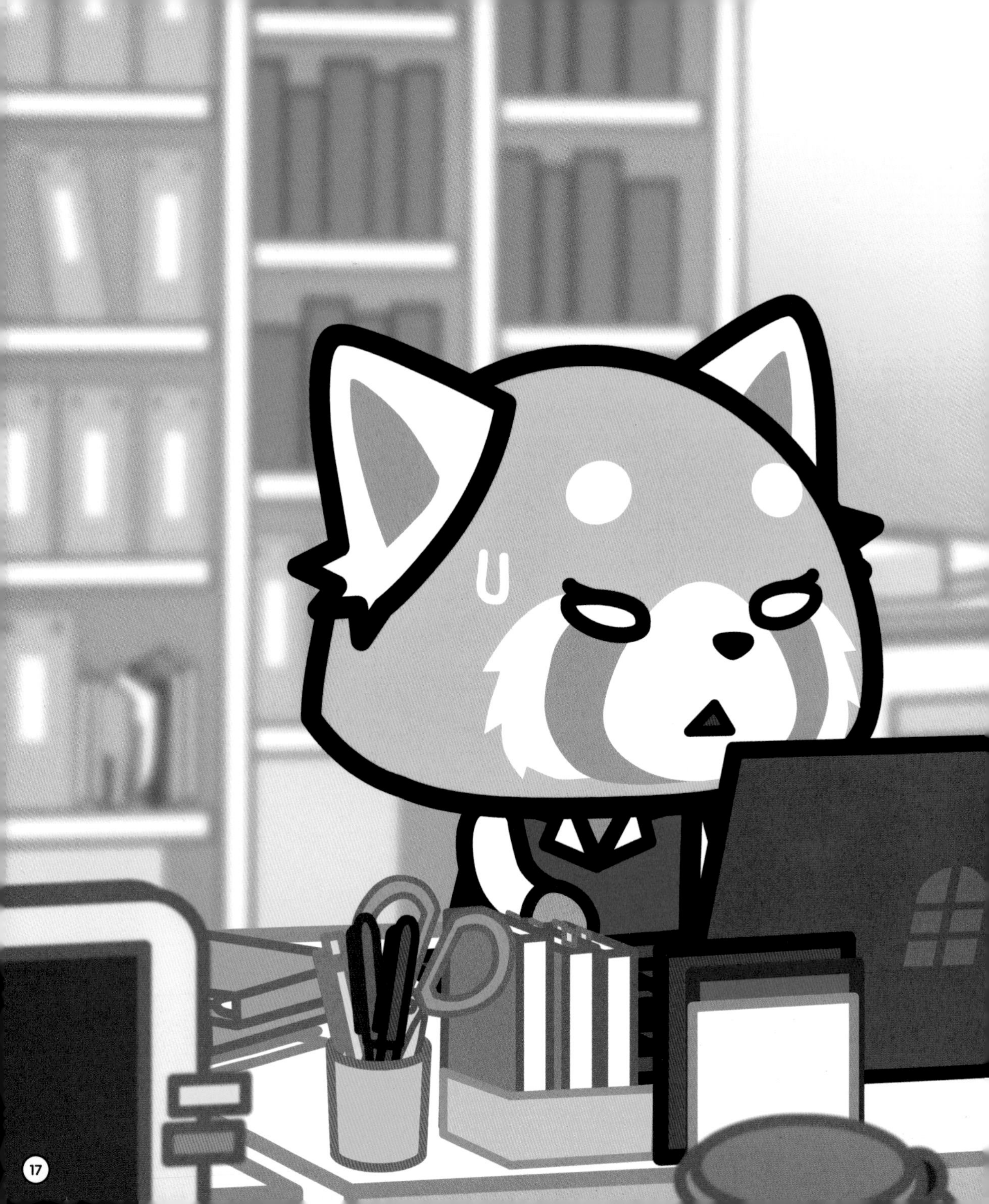

CHAPTER TWO: OFFICE LIFE

Congratulations! You made it to work. Now you have to face the office. Ugh. From navigating the pitfalls of lunchroom conversation to teasing out the meaning behind meaningless corporate jargon to planning the holiday office party, I've done it all and am here to help. Life in the corporate job lane isn't as easy—or as mindless—as it looks. You've gotta stay on your toes and stay positive even if your boss is a pig, or your colleague has drunk herself into dreamland at an after-hours company outing —again—or the only thing that stands between you and the flu virus is the flimsy cubicle wall that separates you from your lung-hacking, tissue-clutching colleague.

Remember: even if your boss is a jerk, any time out with him/her is an opportunity to score brownie points. That said, sometimes avoiding colleagues after work is better than joining them. PowerPoint is an art form. Hand sanitizer saves lives. Photocopying your best "I-can't-take-it-anymore" resting face is ten times more satisfying than taking a selfie. (Trust me.) There's a lot to remember and it's hard to keep smiling when you're surrounded by so many imbeciles. Here's a tip: staying positive means staying caffeinated.

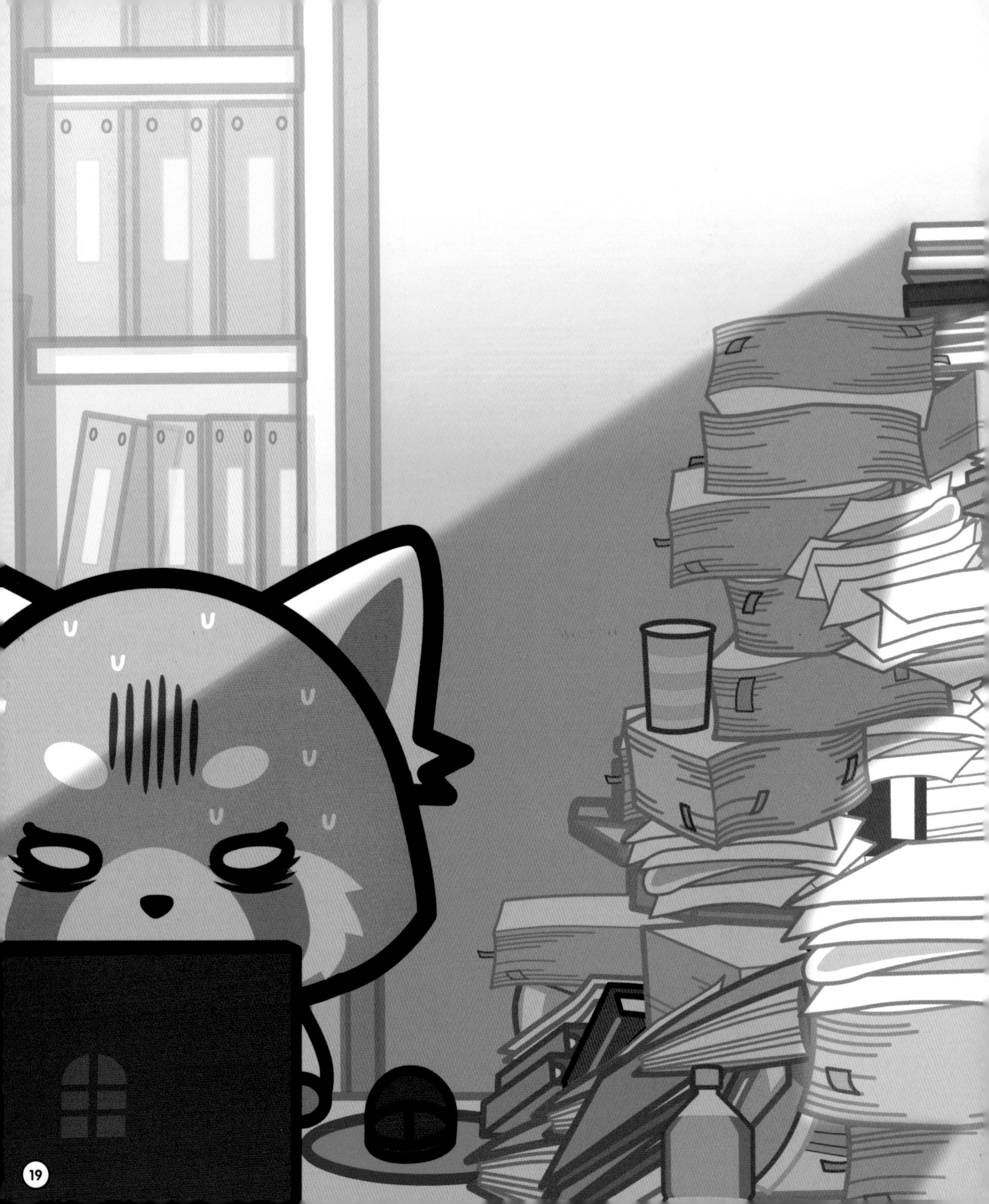

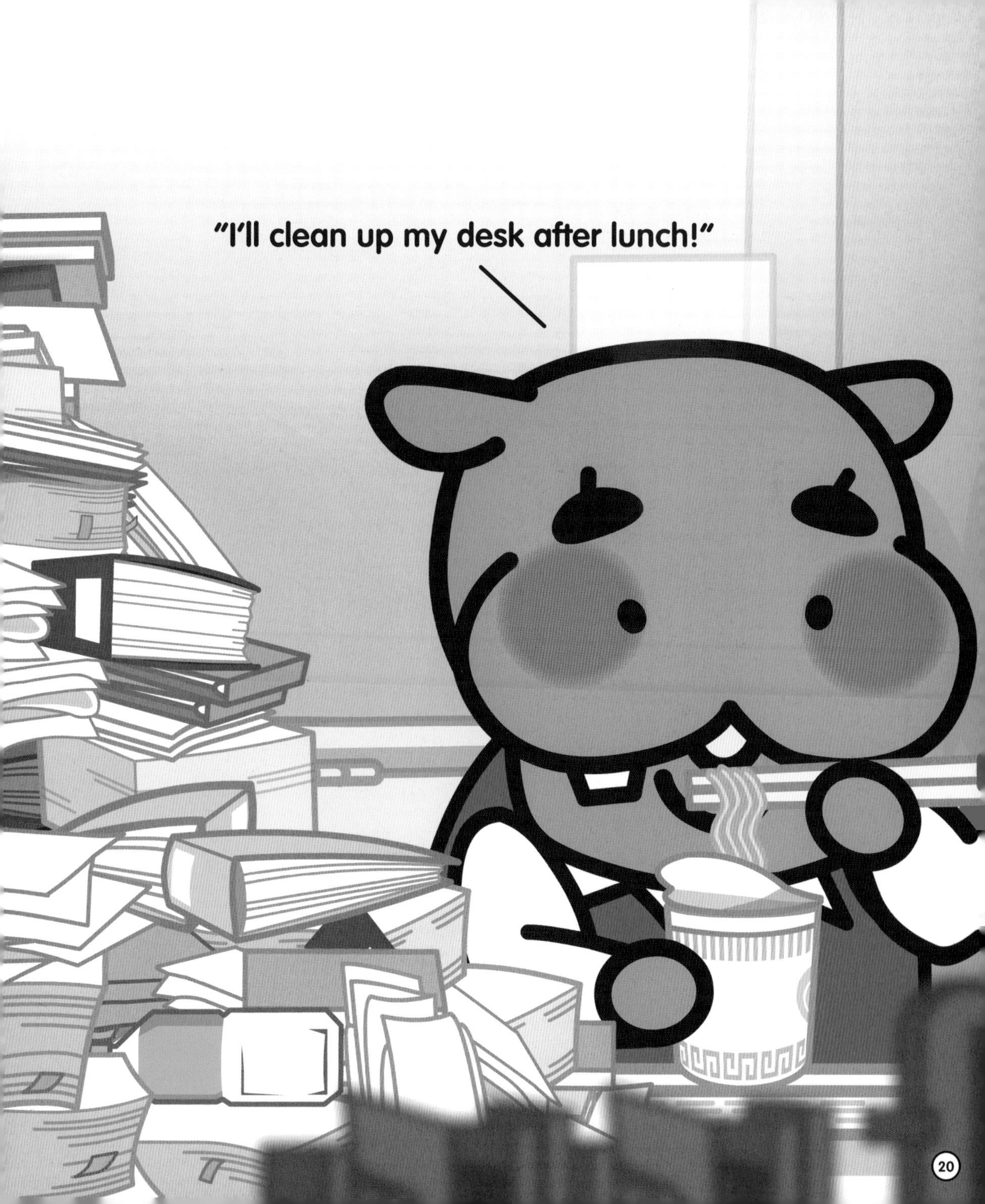
"I'll clean up my desk after lunch!"

OFFICE AC BATTLE

When you and a fellow colleague are engaged in a battle for the ages—namely, who controls the AC—it's wise to let cooler heads prevail. I, however, am not one of those cooler heads. What can I say: some just like it hot (or at least 65 degrees, which is a totally normal temperature for all employees to be comfortable). If your colleague is the kind of person who wears flip-flops during the wintertime and cranks the AC to Ice Age levels, I recommend that you exercise your right to rage. Two can play at this game. When he goes low, you go high . . . and raise the temperature settings. And if the constant back and forth doesn't warm you up, your anger will make you feel positively cozy! (If all else fails, go practical: a sweater for you and a fan for him. Just don't let him see you sweat.)

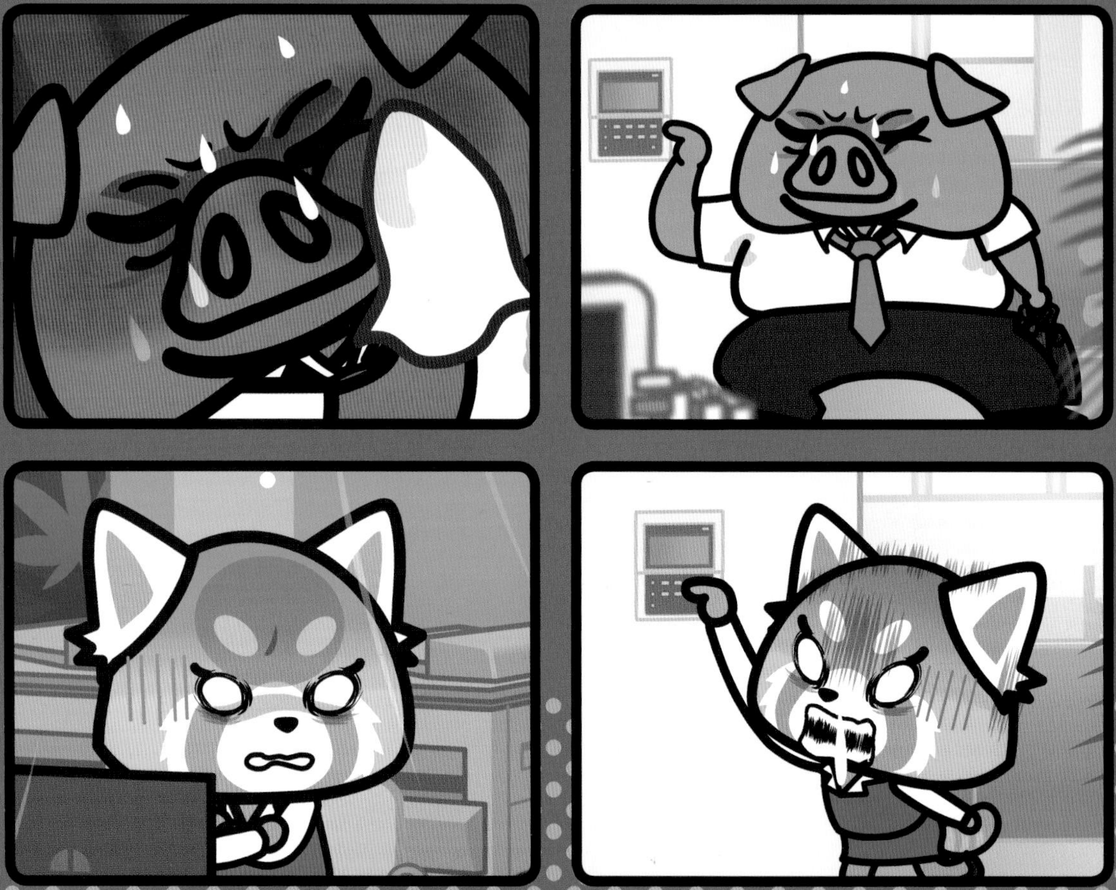

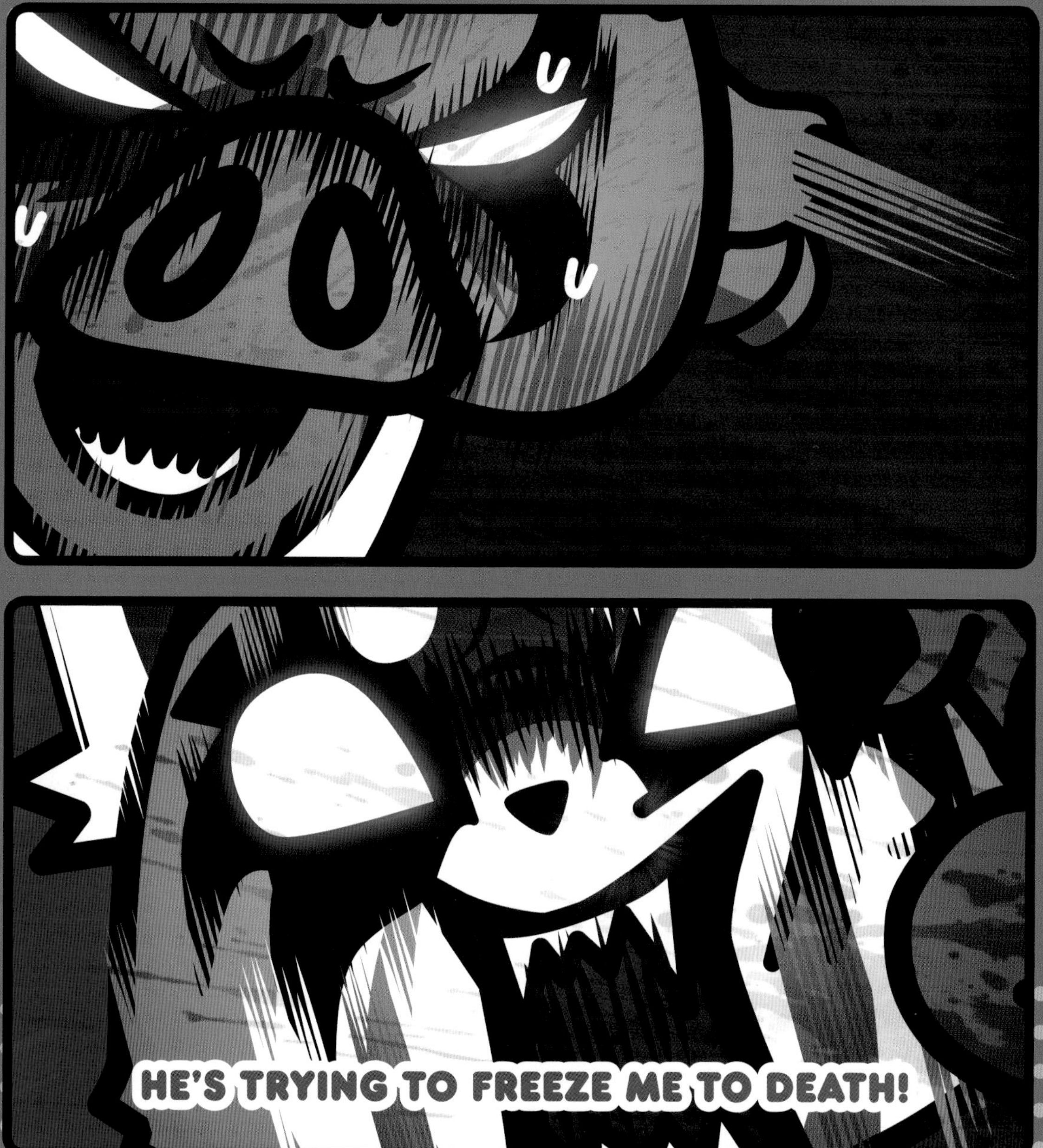
HE'S TRYING TO FREEZE ME TO DEATH!

TIP If you want something stapled right, staple it yourself!

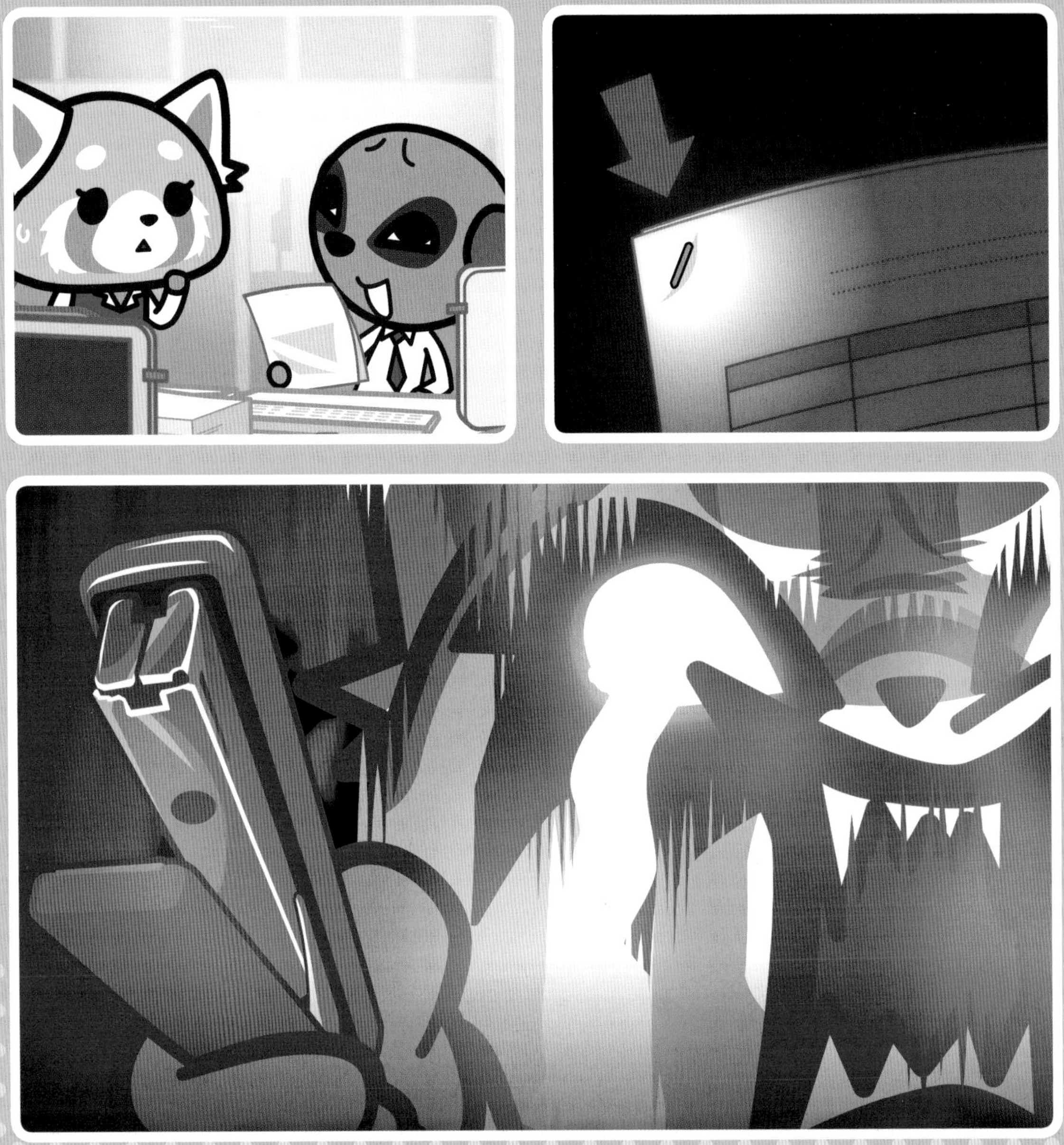

TIP If you're sick, you better stay home! We don't want your germs.

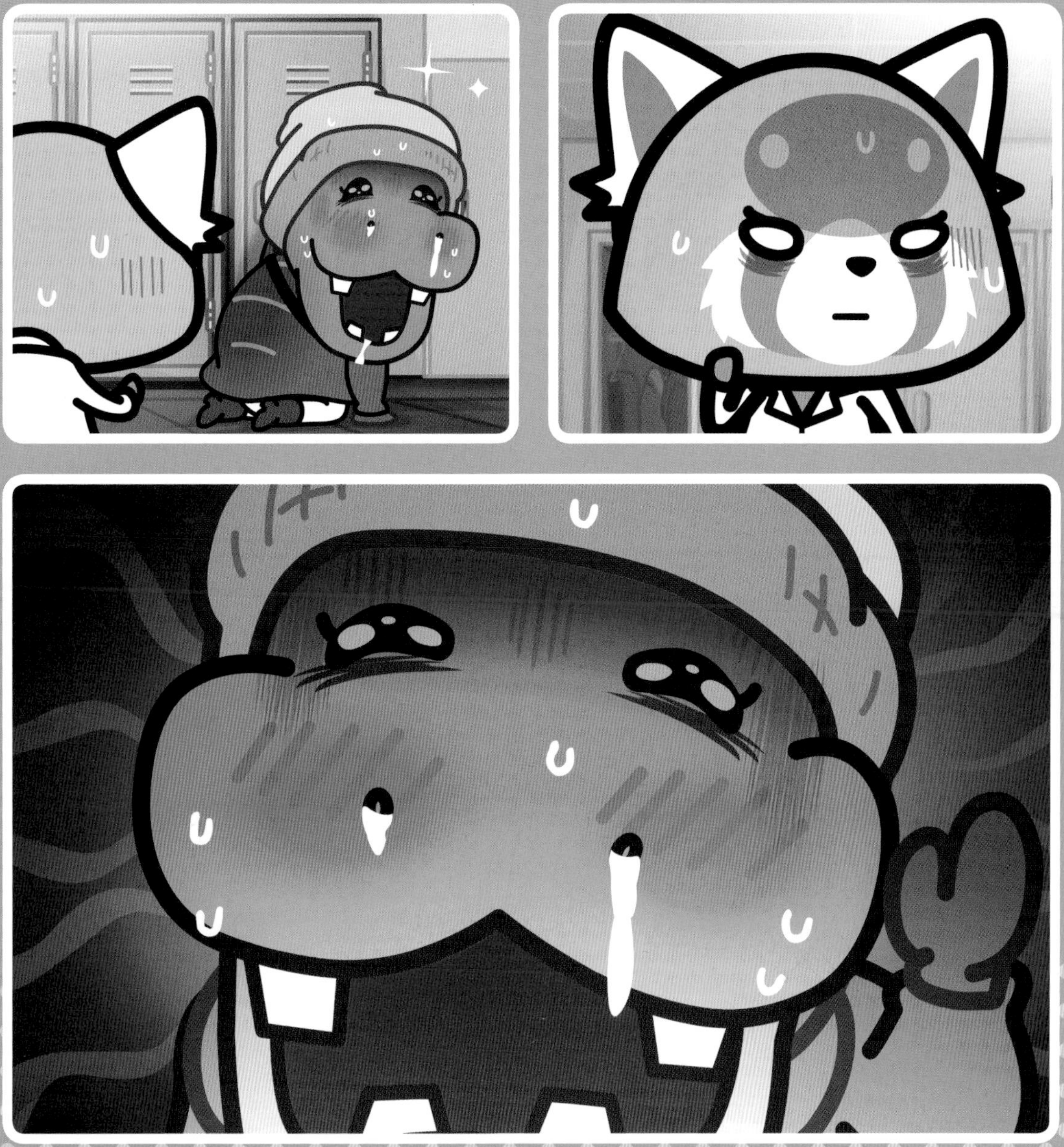

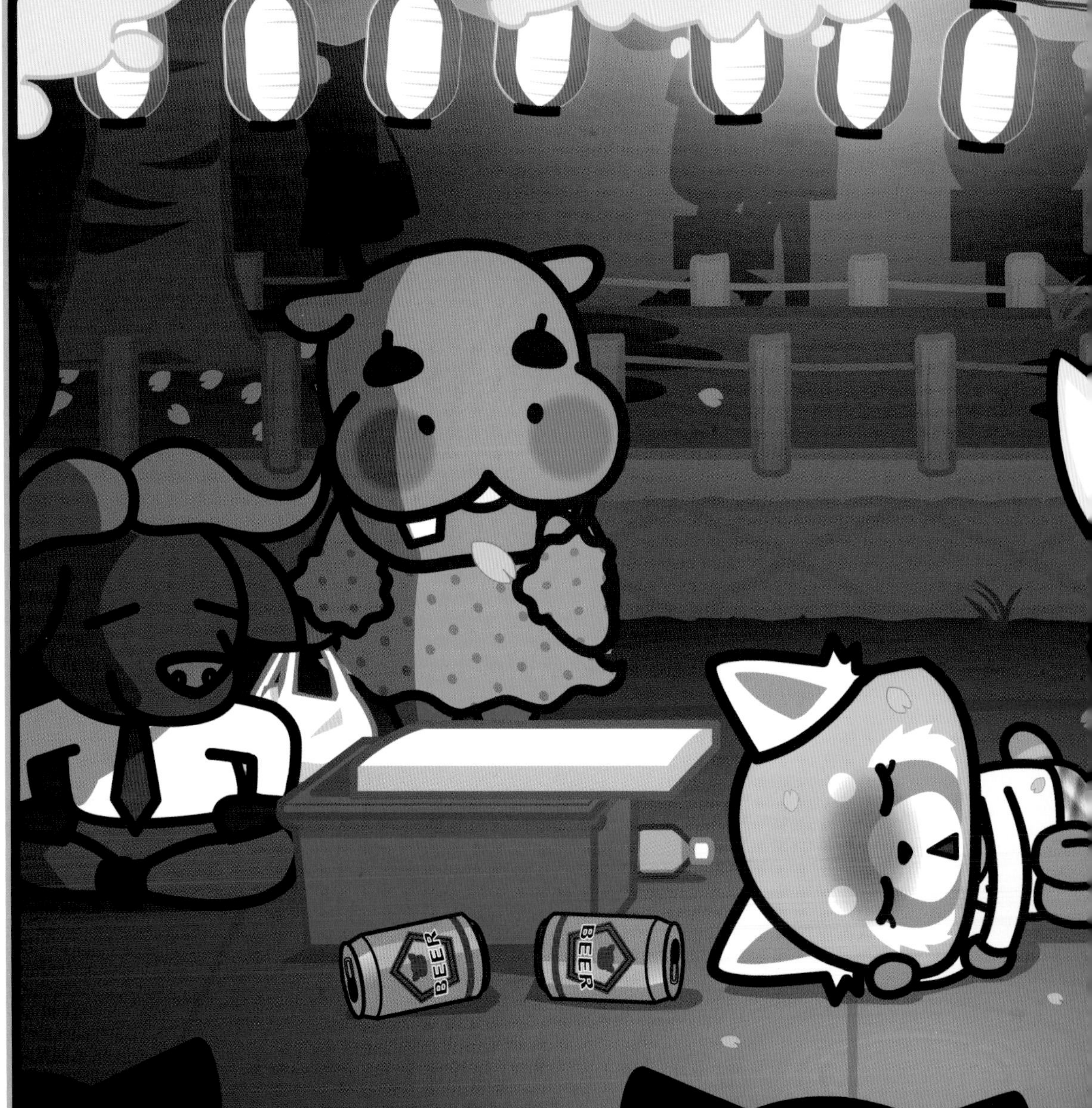
BEER
BEER

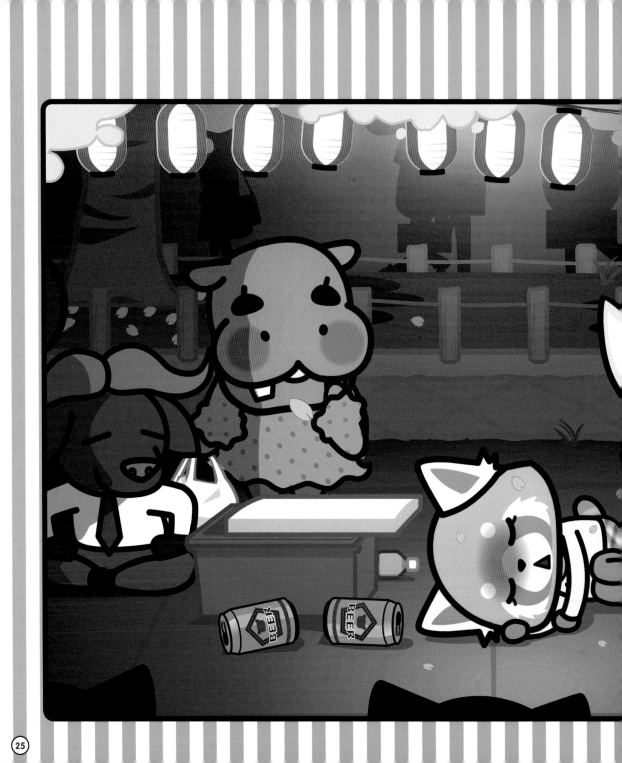

PLANNING A COMPANY PARTY

I'm the go-to gal for company parties, and have planned everything from off-site birthday celebrations and baby showers to summer BBQs and retirement shindigs. It can be tempting, when planning a party, to make it convenient for you. It should go without saying but if your friend is a vegan and you're planning her birthday party, don't book the irresistible chicken restaurant located a mere five-minute-walk from your train station. The most important thing to remember is: the party isn't for you.

Trust me: the most successful party is one where the guest of honor is treated, well, honorably, and his or her likes and dislikes are respected. It's a little trickier when you're planning a large group get-together like the annual company summer BBQ. In these situations, it's best to play to the masses, and arrange a variety of activities or bring different types of food for everyone to enjoy. And if that fails, there's always beer and karaoke.

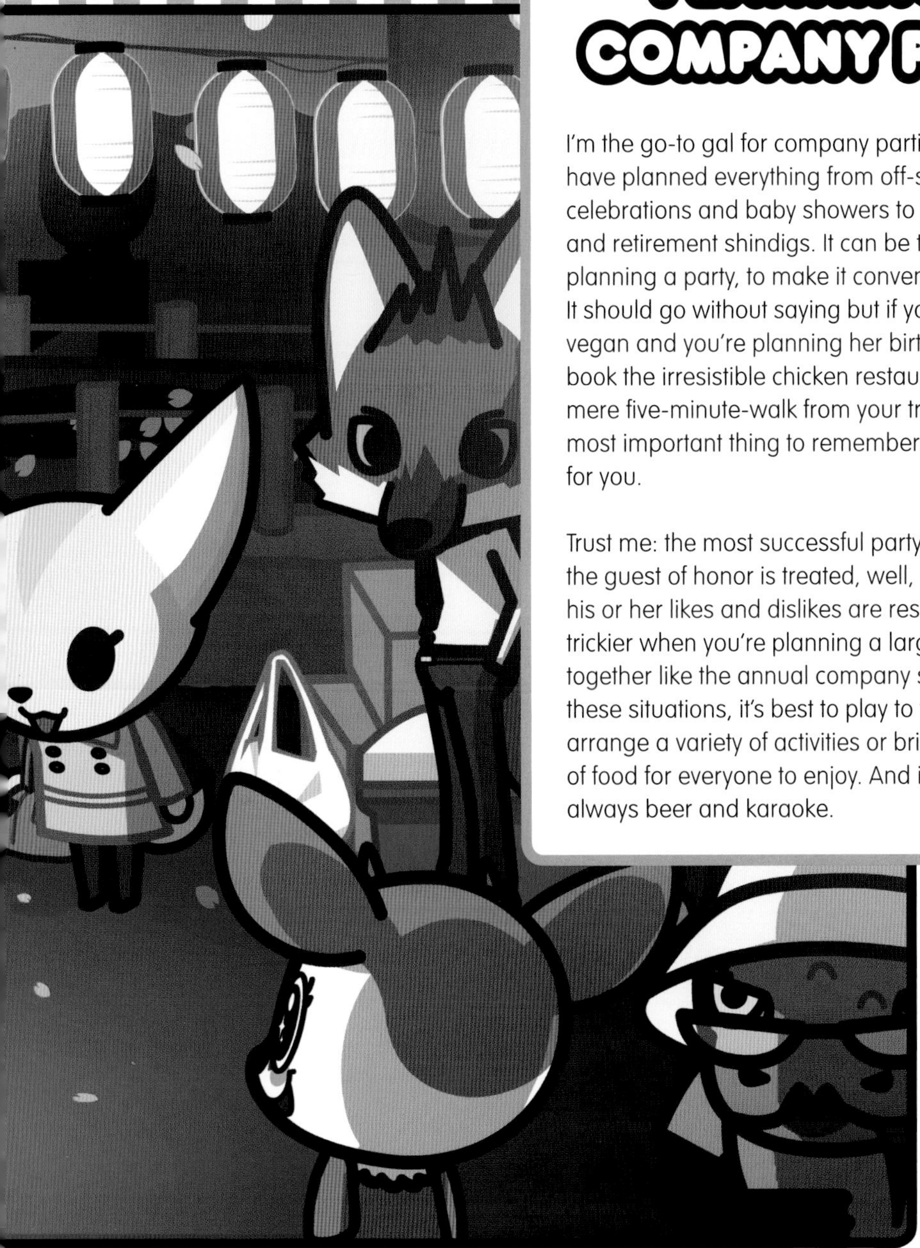

LUNCH CRASHER

It's lunchtime. Do you know where your boss is? If he's sitting next to you, having pulled up a chair to "hang" with you and his staff, a word of warning: don't make eye contact. Also, your salad is now your life vest. Eat it as though it's a culinary wonder; it literally takes your breath away. If he doesn't get the hint and yammers on and on, you could try releasing the rage. Even if you don't actually voice the words, your eyes will say it all.

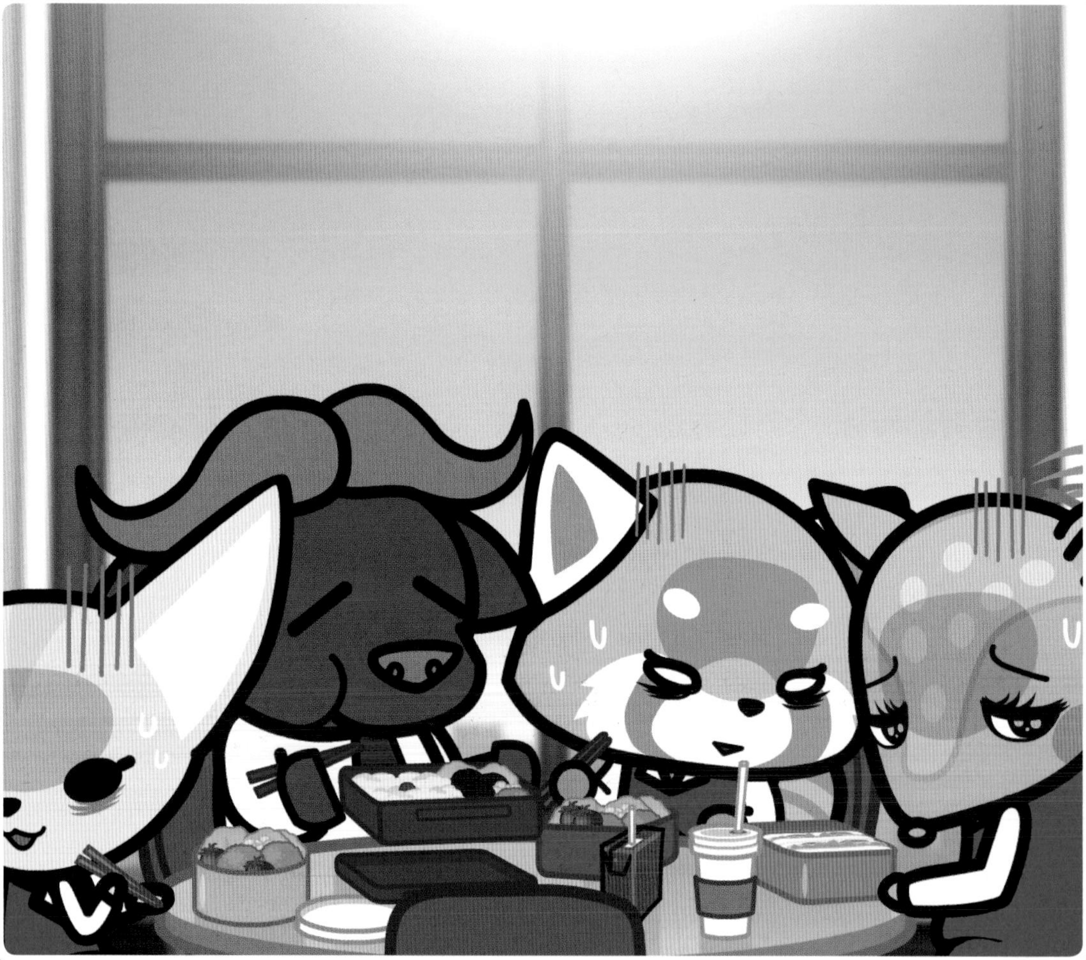

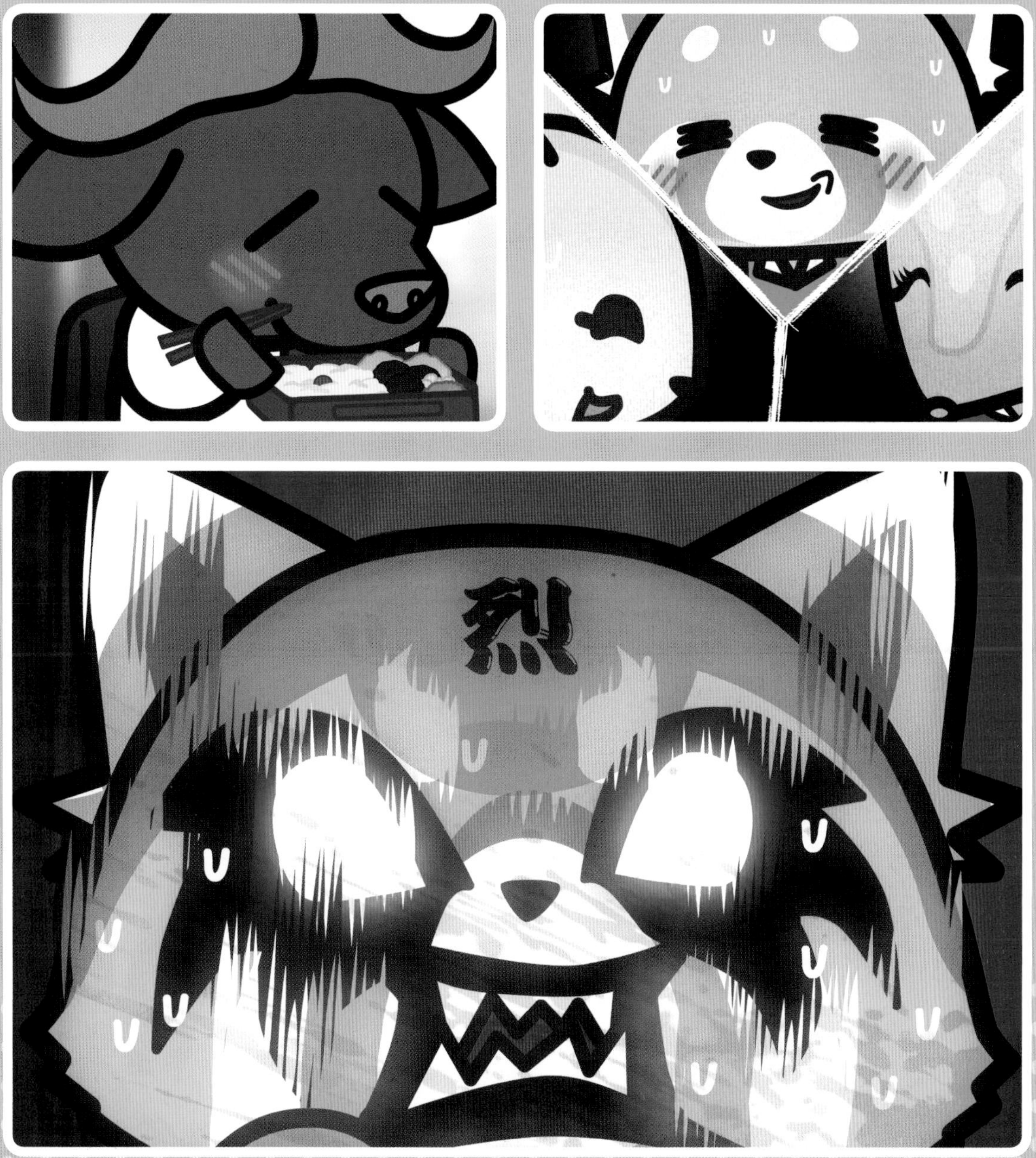
烈

THE MANIPULATOR/ DOUBLE-CROSSER

The manipulator/double-crosser is always at the ready with something cynical to say. She (or he) points out other colleagues' shortcomings but turns on the charm when speaking to the upper brass. Worse, she has no problem belittling her staff.

When dealing with a manipulative double-crosser, I like to employ the age-old yet effective method of Do Not Engage. Listen—passively—only if you must. Don't argue or rationalize the double-crossers behavior. Remember, a manipulator can only manipulate you if you participate. Don't take the bait. If you've successfully survived another workday, congratulate yourself. And if that means stopping off for some fried chicken and cocktails, go ahead: guzzle up like the boss you are.

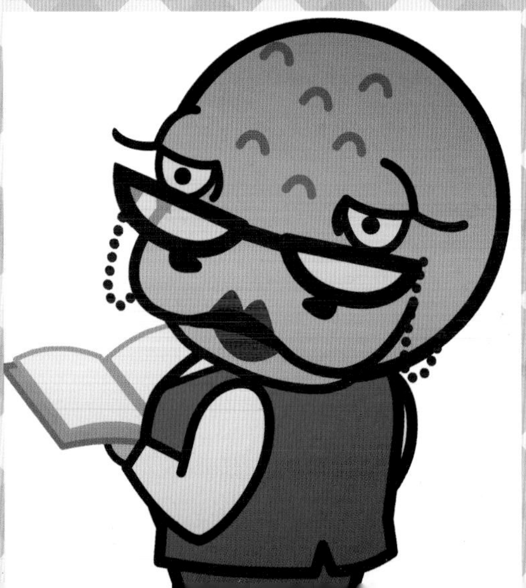

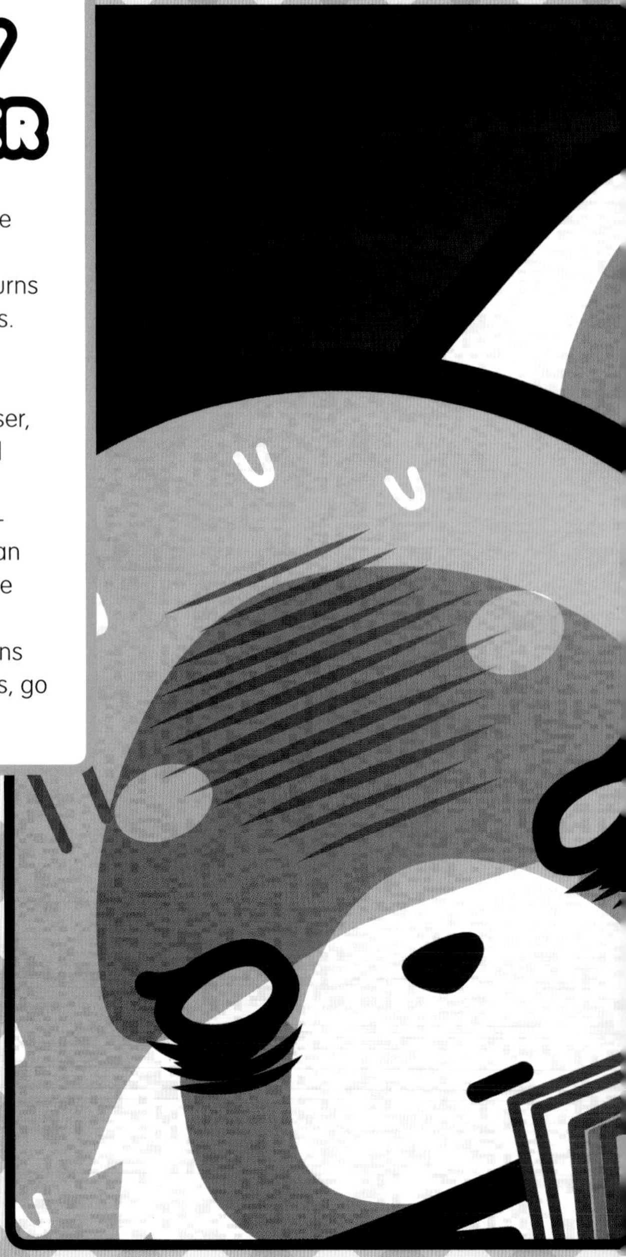

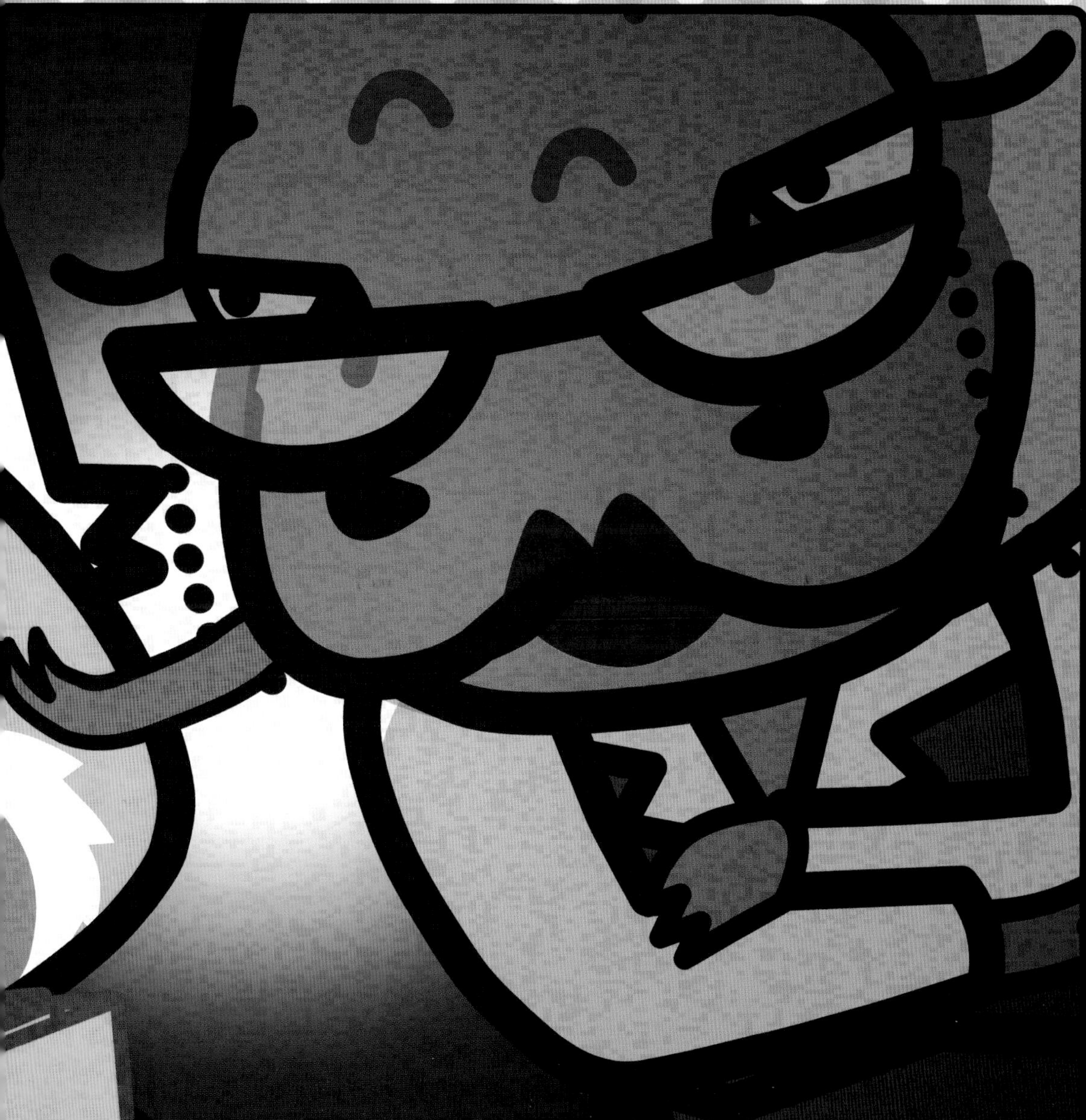

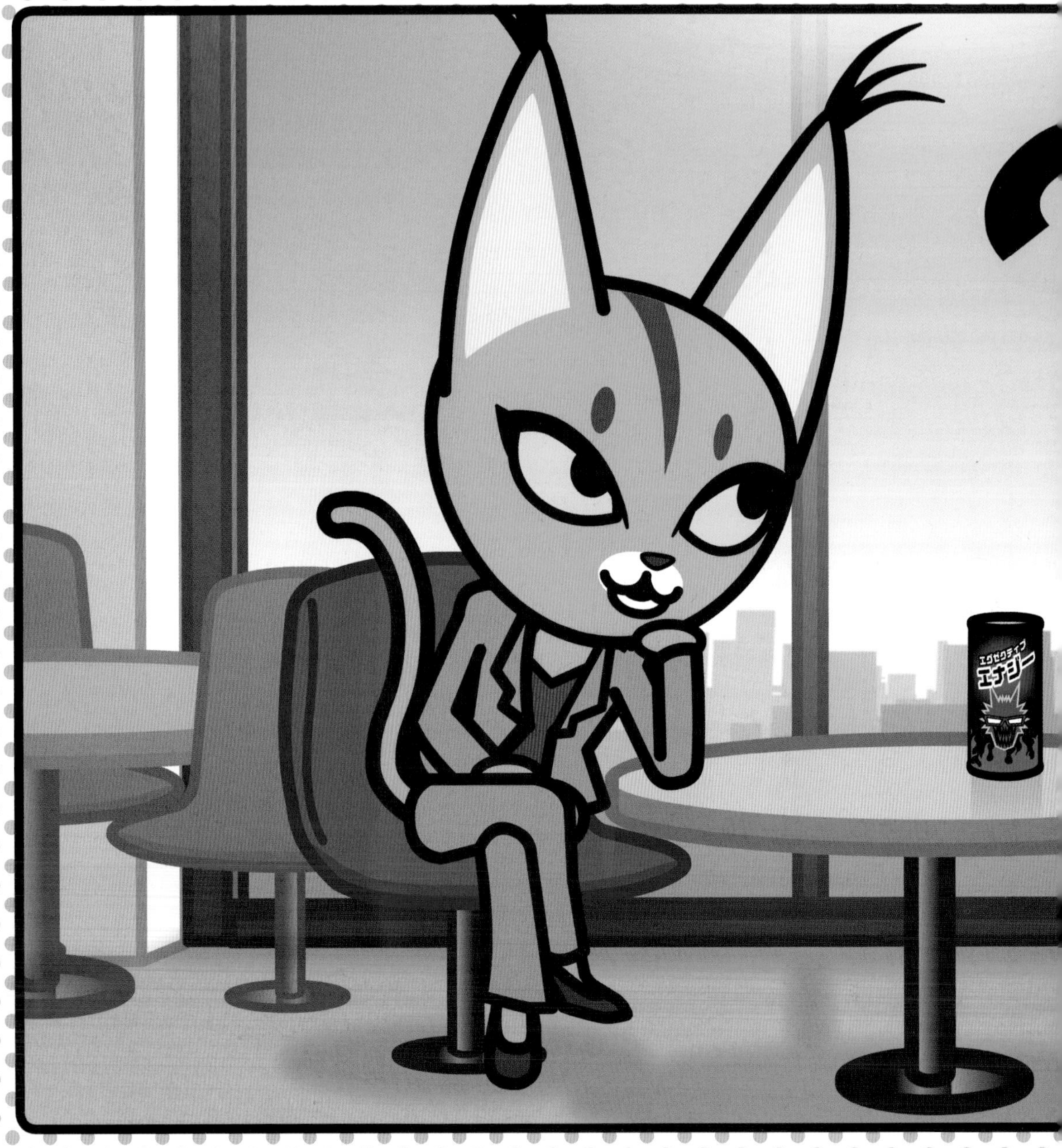
エグゼクティブ
エナジー

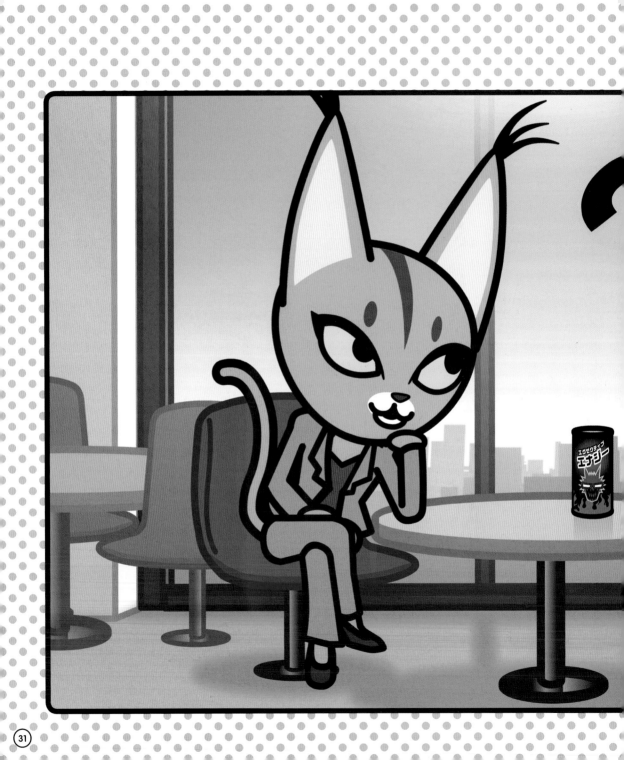

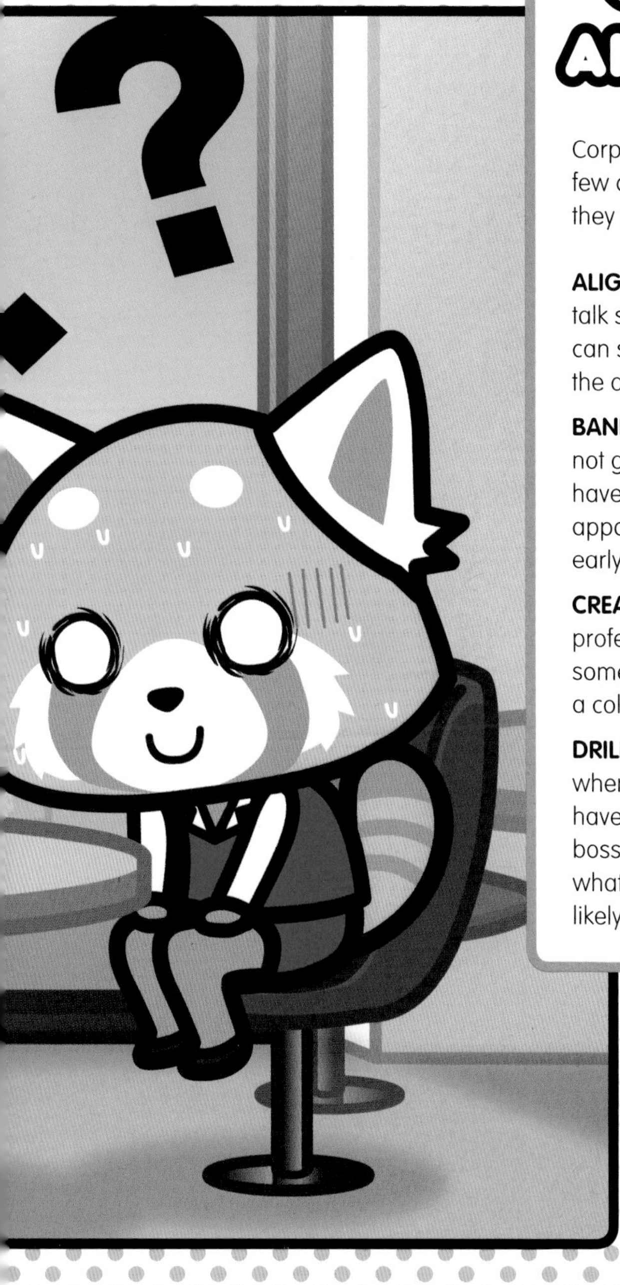

OFFICE JARGON AND TRANSLATION

Corporate speak is its own language. Here are a few common terms and my interpretation of what they mean. Use at your own discretion:

ALIGNMENT: Your plan sucks. Mine is better. Let's talk so we can reach some alignment, i.e., so you can see the error of your ways and worship me like the accounting god I am!

BANDWIDTH: An excuse your colleague uses to not get her work done on time, as in, "I just don't have the bandwidth." Refrain from noting that she apparently had enough bandwidth to leave work early to party until 3 in the morning.

CREATIVE: This typically refers to something a professional designer worked on but is usually just something I put together by photocopying together a collage of file reports in different colors.

DRILL DOWN: Figure out what went wrong, when, where, and by whom. Hint: when you're going to have a meeting with your boss to "drill down" and fix what happened, *you're* most likely the "thing" getting fixed.

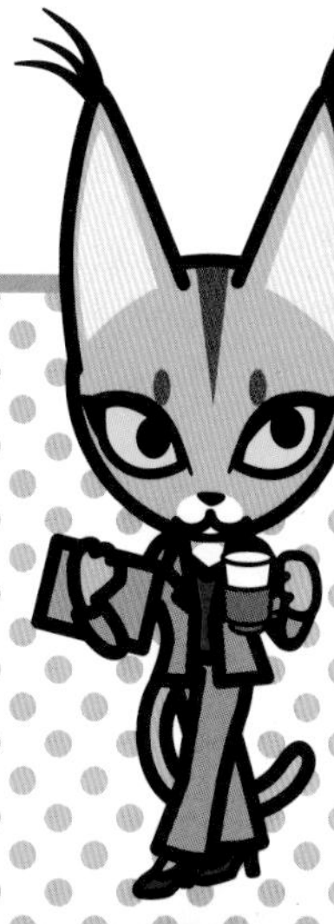

MAKE YOUR DESK A HAPPY PLACE

t can't be all rage all the time. Sometimes it's nice o talk a walk on the sunny side of life and spruce ıp your office space. A nice flower vase is a little nvestment that can work wonders on your mental state. Whenever I get upset at work all I have to do s look at the flower on my desk to go back to my happy place.

Just ignore the sticky price tag that, no matter how many times you SCRATCH it, WON'T COME OFF OH MY GOD *who makes these things anyway?!* Let's see . . . I can either Keep Calm and Scratch On or I can declare war.

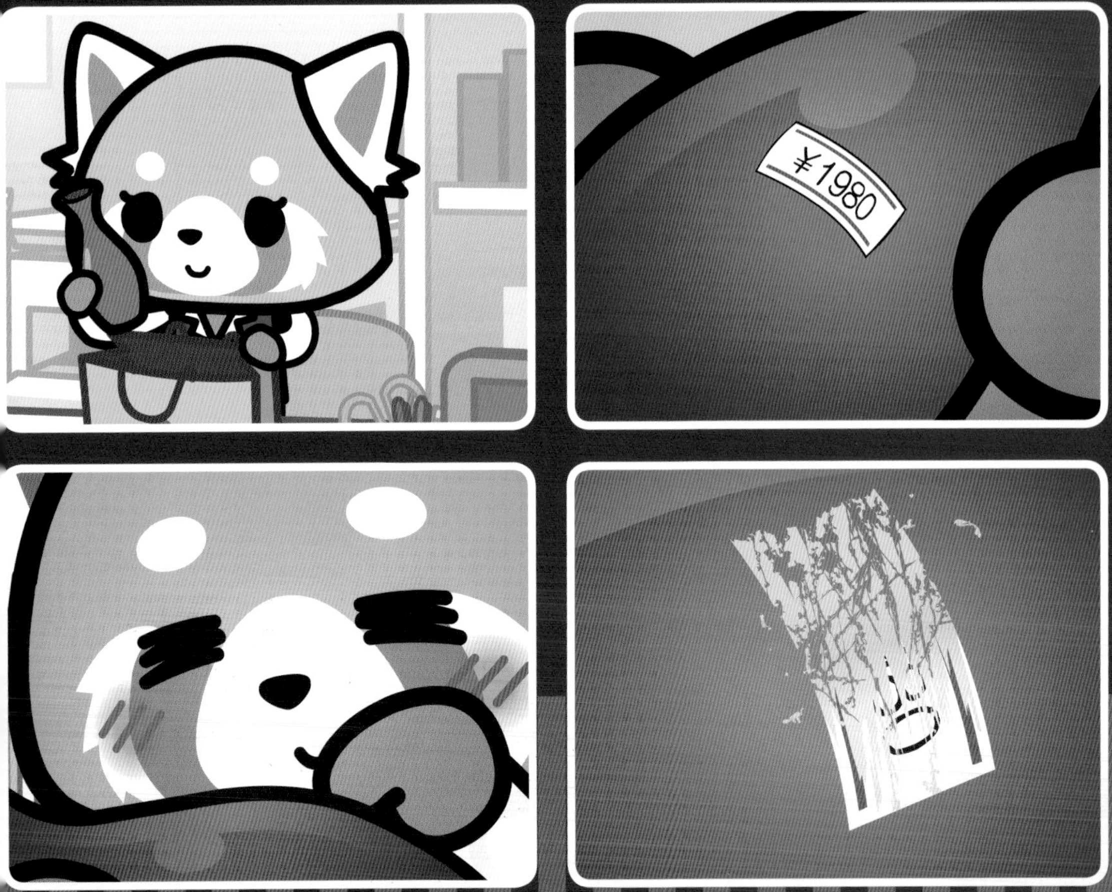
¥1980

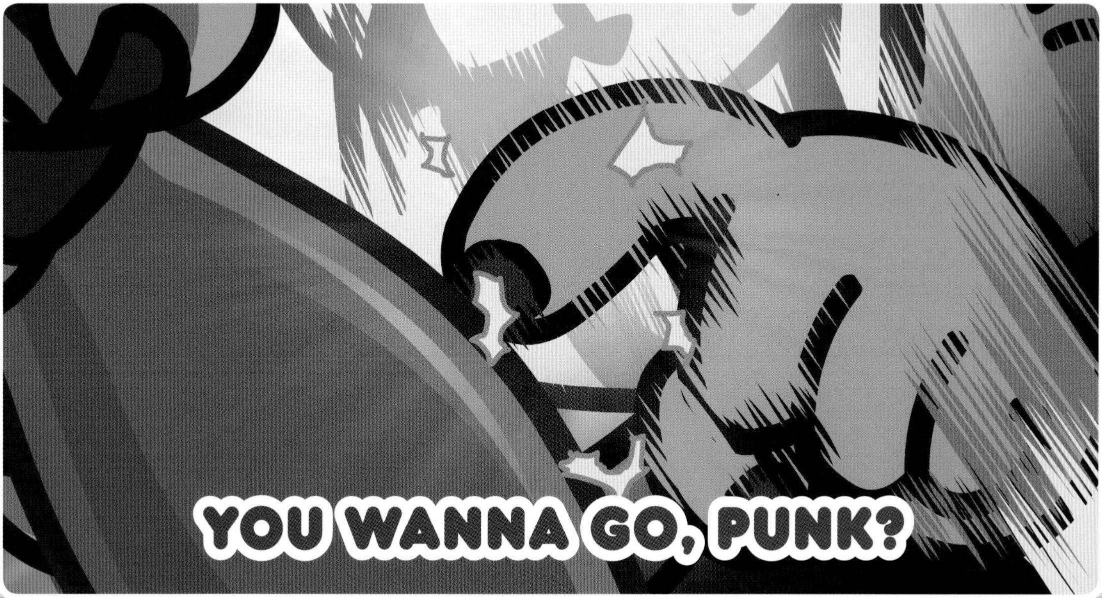
YOU WANNA GO, PUNK?

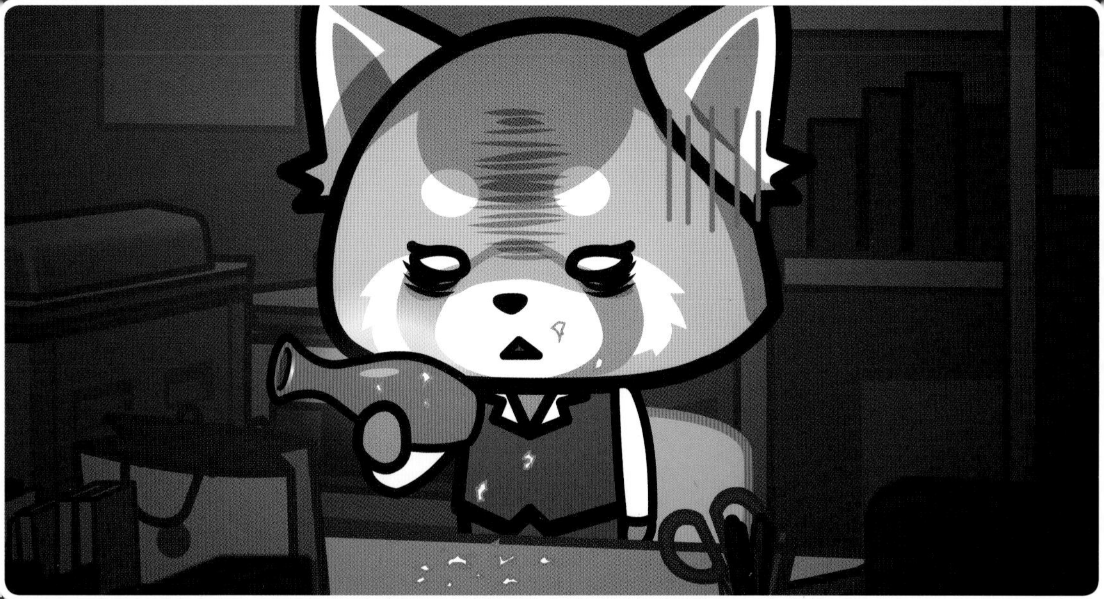

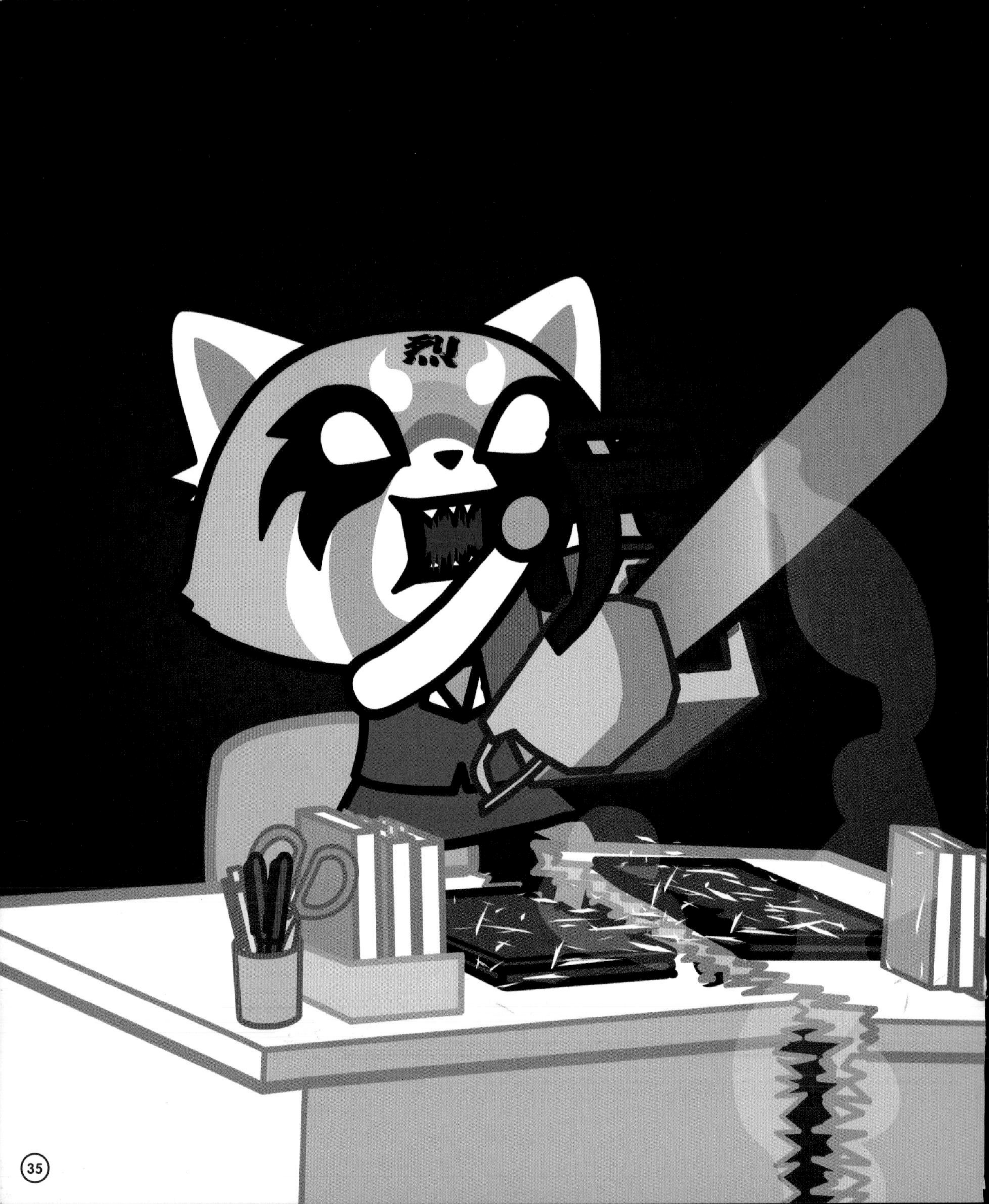
烈

CHAPTER THREE: EMBRACE THE RAGE AND CARRY ON

The rage is real. There are any number of reasons the rage may hit you like a bolt of lightning—you lend a beloved book to a work colleague who uses it like her personal table mat, getting crumbs in the spine, greasy fingerprints on the jacket, and writing notes to herself in ink in the margins; you call the IT staff person to fix your computer and, instead, he breaks your office chair, telephone, and desk, and, no, the computer STILL doesn't work; someone had the gall to take your lunch from the office fridge, and now you're starving and cranky.

For any one of these situations, there's an accompanying way to rage. Lucky for you, I've broken down some methods in this chapter. Remember: there's a little rage inside all of us. The most accomplished rage machines among us know how to harness the madness and unleash the fire to blaze a new trail forward.

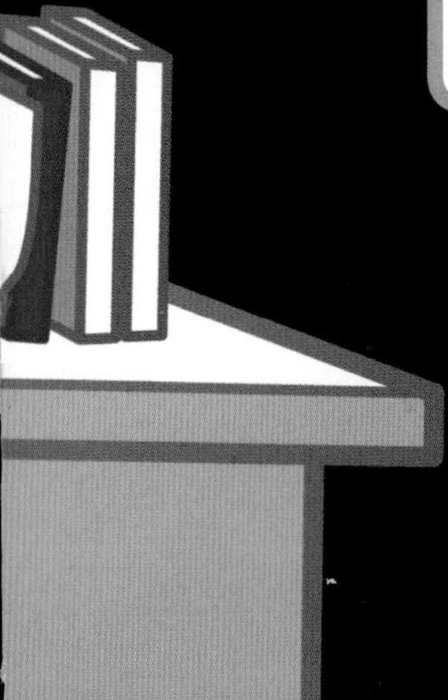

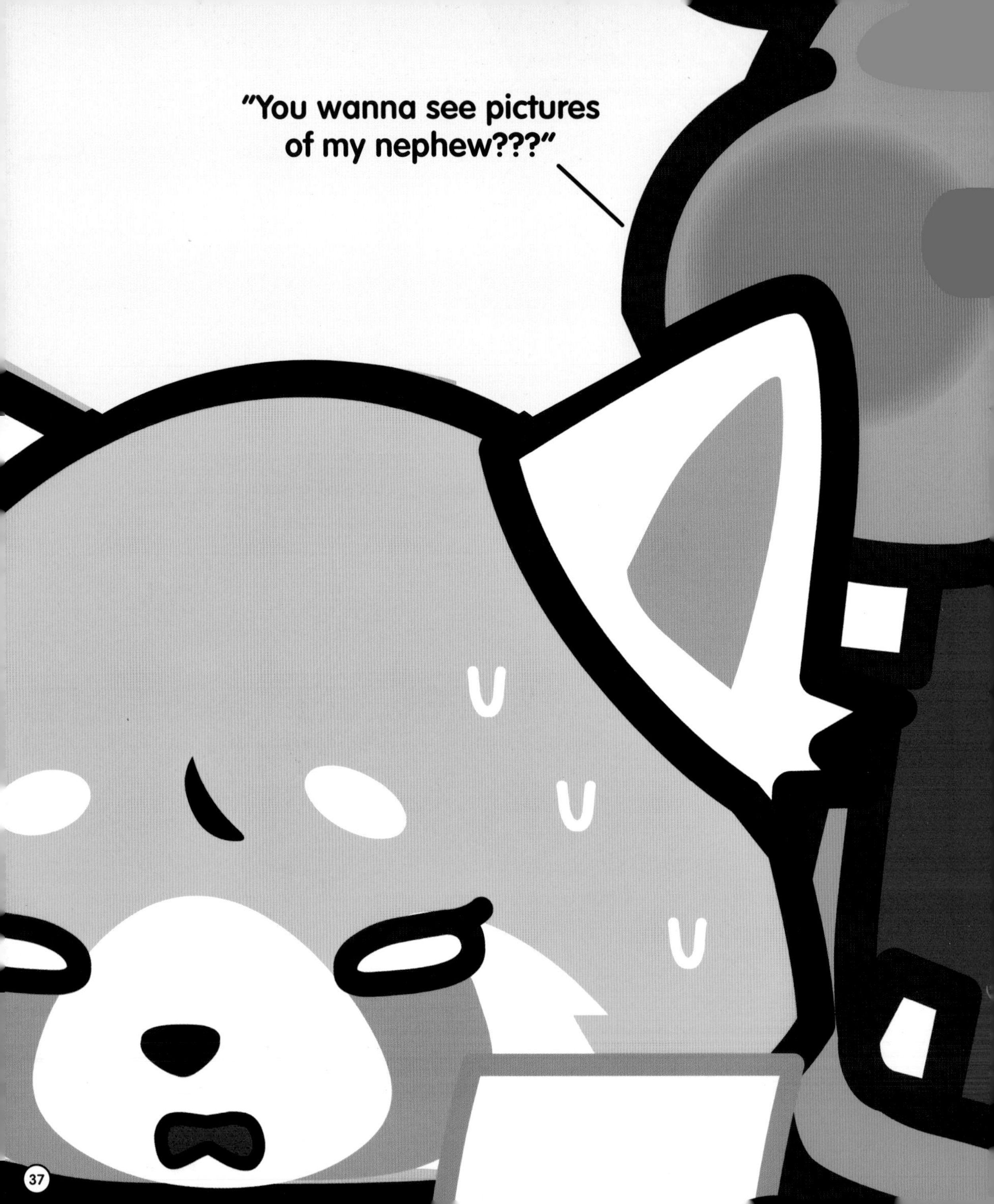
"You wanna see pictures of my nephew???"

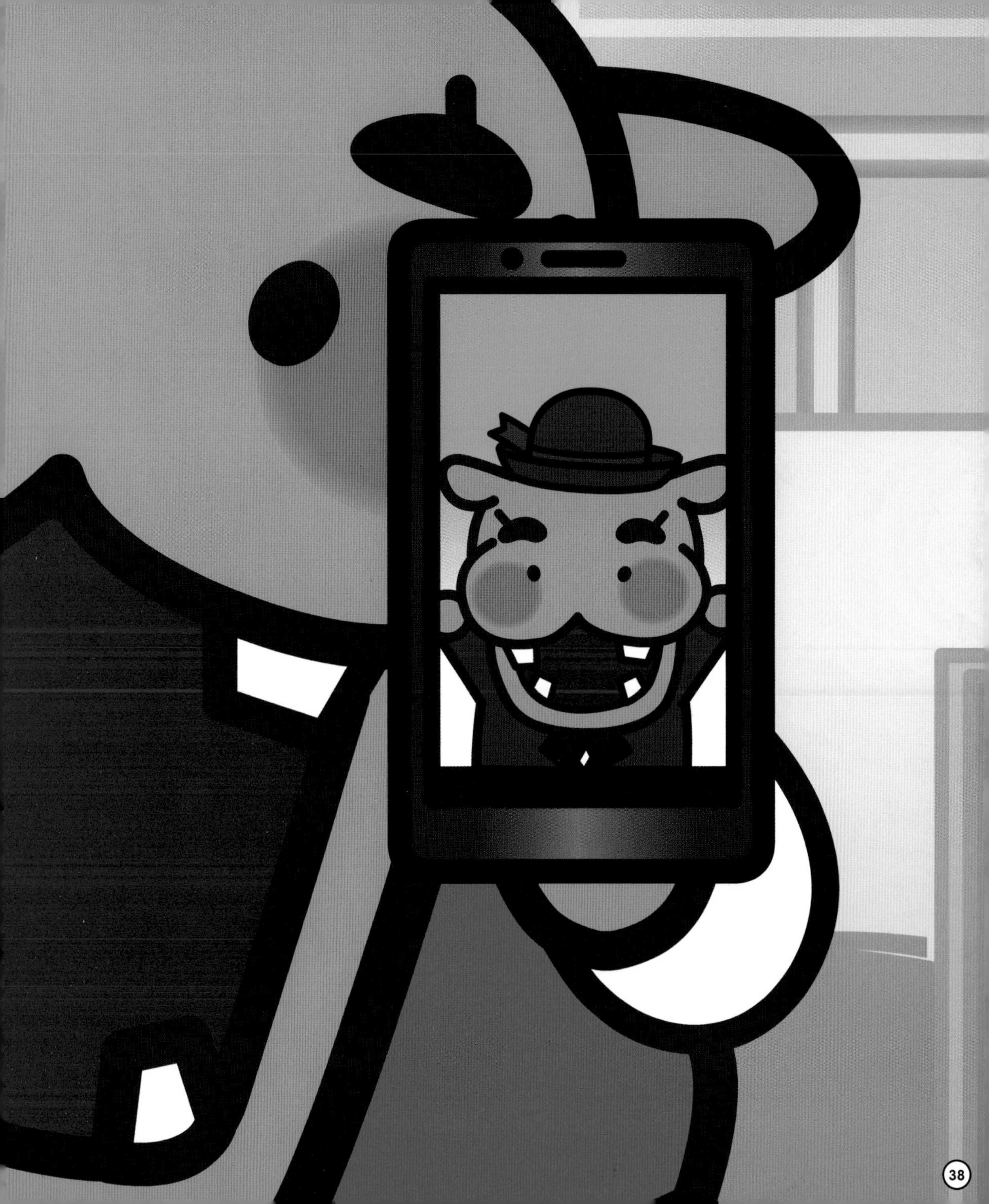

THE ANGRY EMPLOYEE

In my office, Director Ton is the employee who can't get a grip on his anger. He huffs and puffs and even though he's a pig, he thinks he can blow the office down. His violent mood swings keeps everyone walking on eggshells. It's his way or the highway. He's the stodgy, set-in-his-ways guy in the office everyone avoids.

A few words about the difference between his anger and my rage: While rage can be an extreme expression of anger, I don't hold onto it. It surfaces, I rage, and it's gone. Director Ton is always angry. If he only knew the benefits of a good, hard-core thrash metal song. When dealing with an angry employee, it's best to step gingerly, and if his anger tips your point of rage, keep your cool. There's no point in adding more fuel to an out-of-control fire.

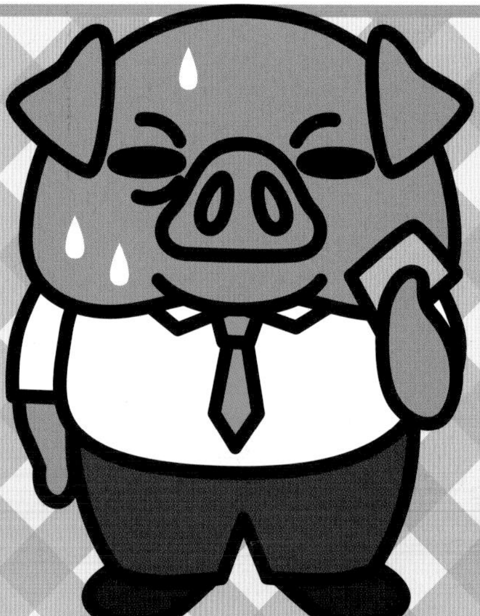

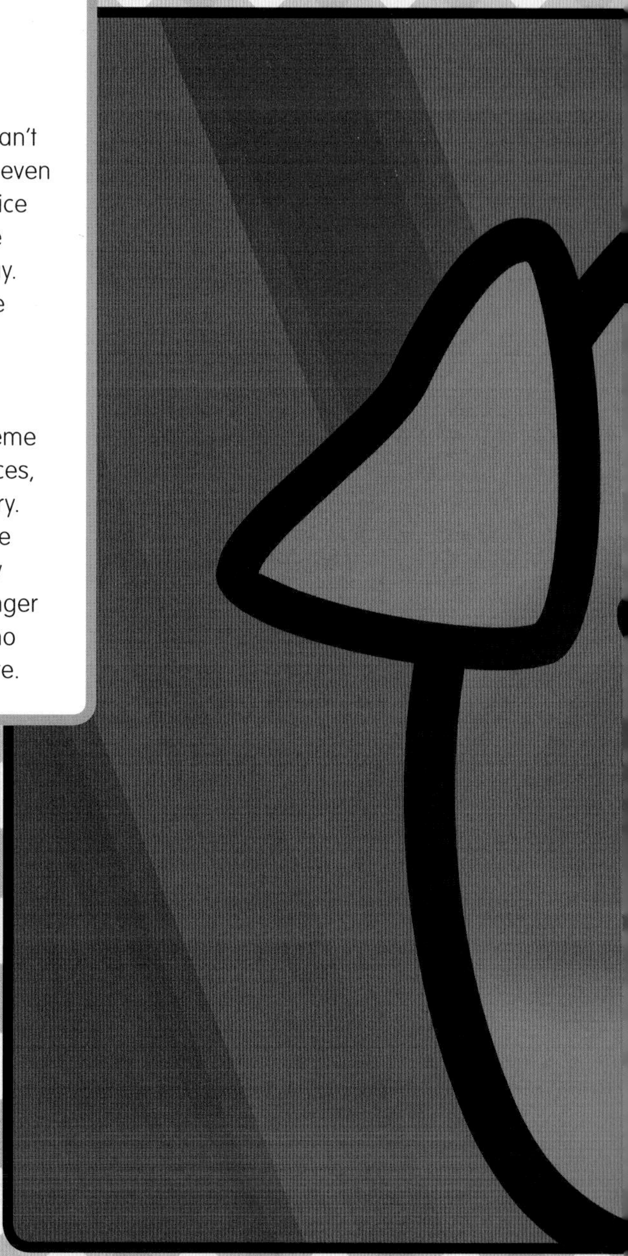

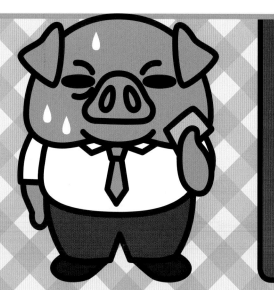

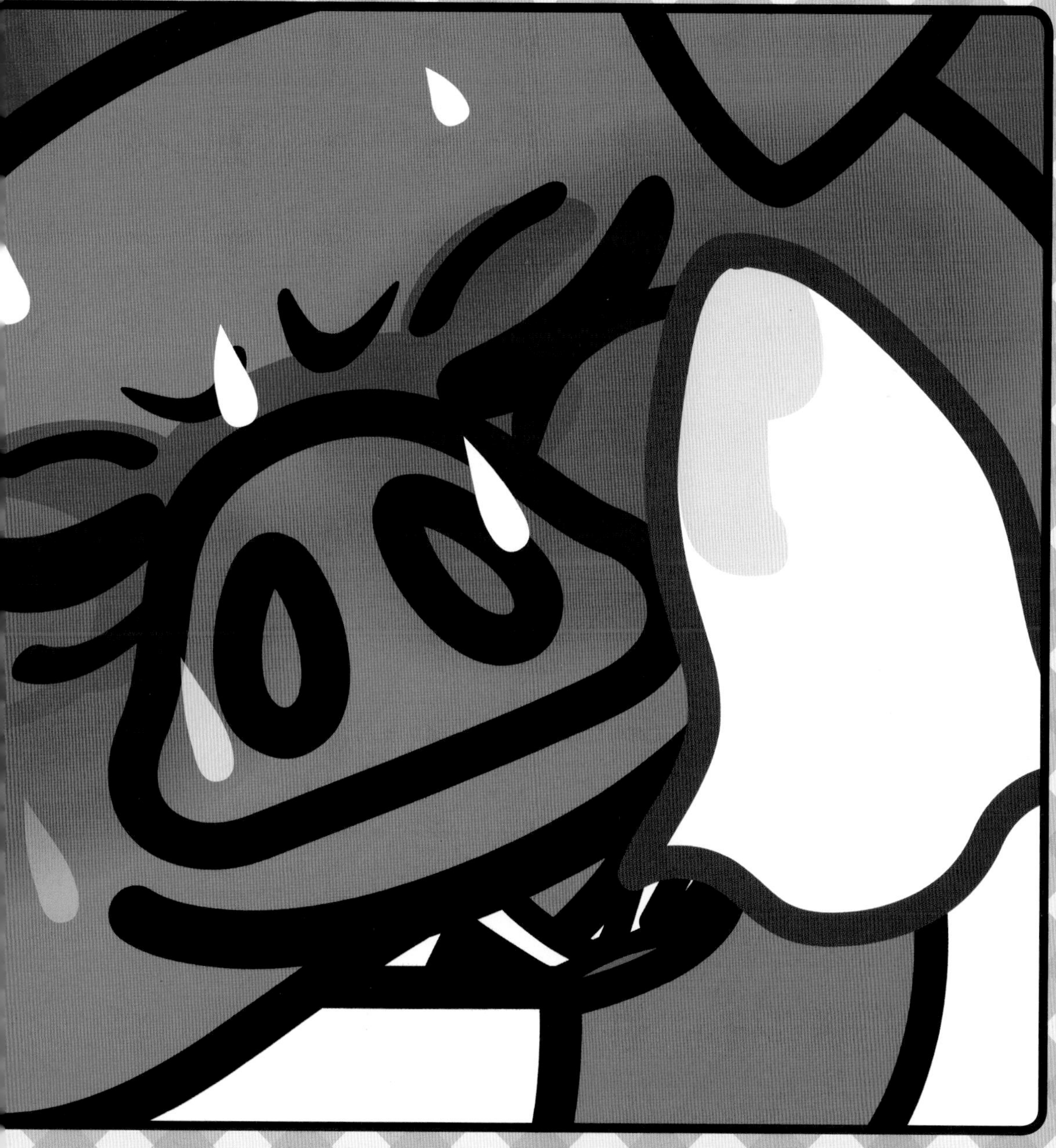

THE EIGHT STEPS OF RAGING

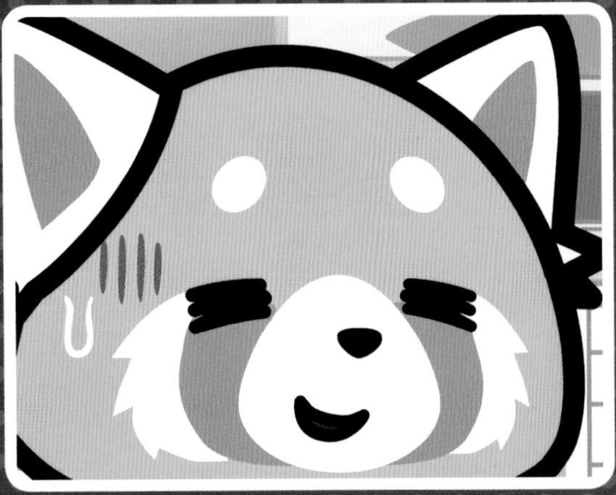

1) Sweat drops begin

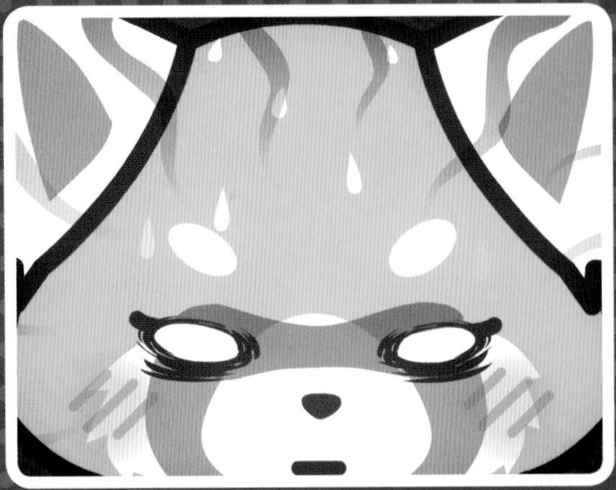

2) Cheeks flush

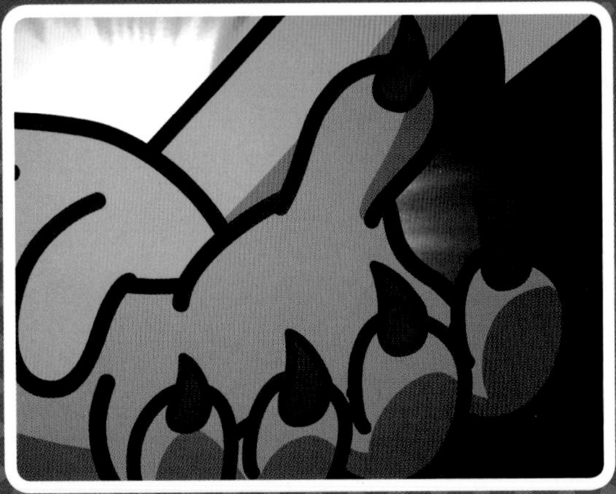

5) Claws pop out

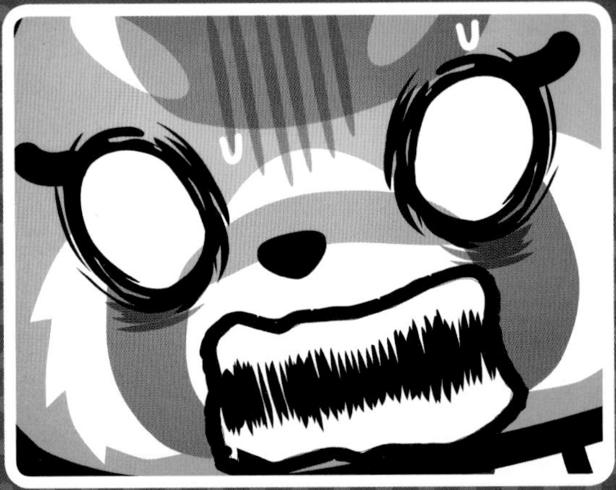

6) Teeth sharpen

3) Forehead throbs

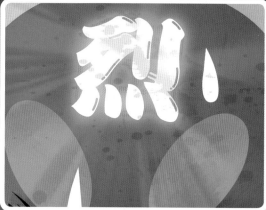

4) Rage mark illuminates

7) Eyes become possessed

8) Full rage achieved

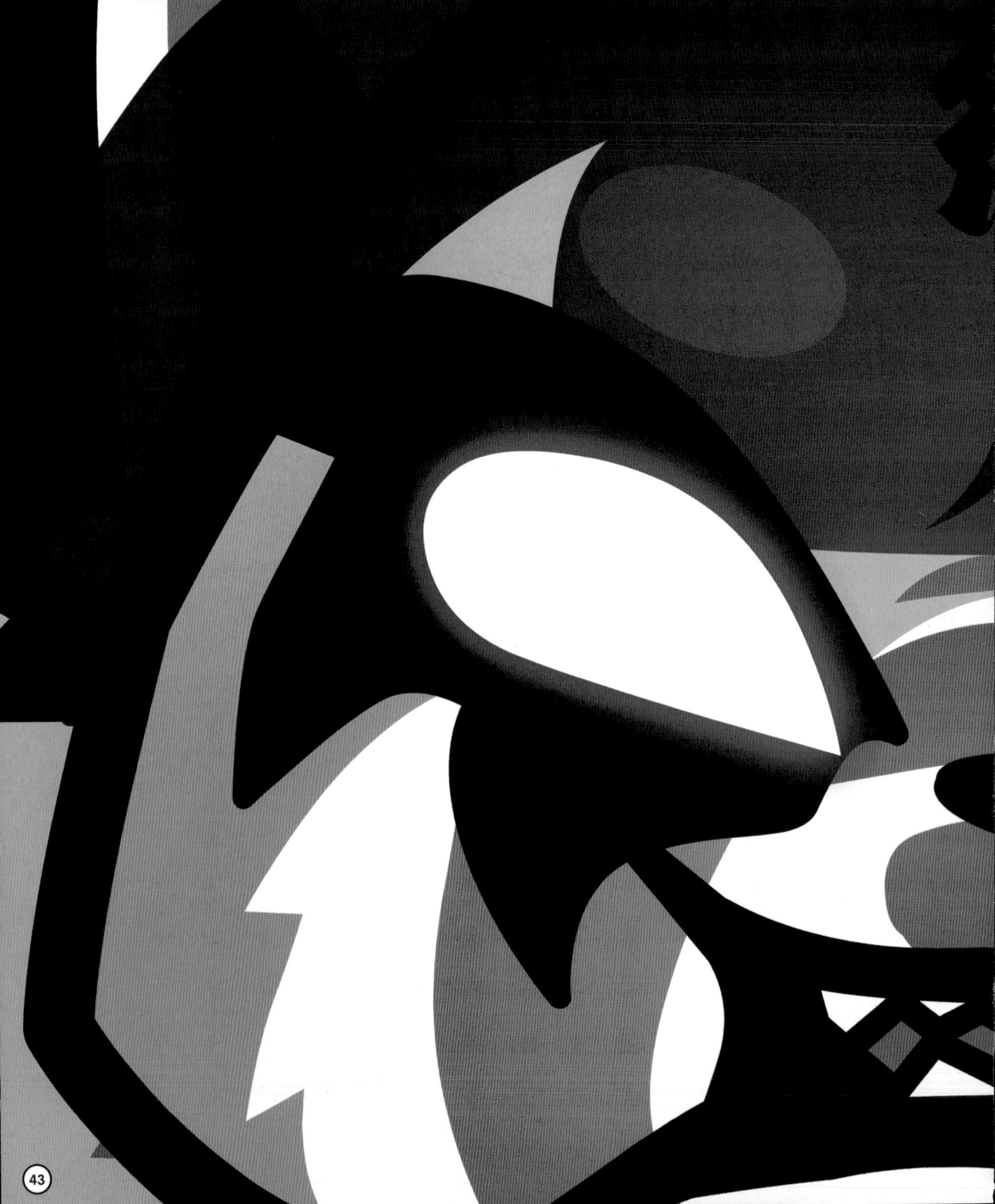

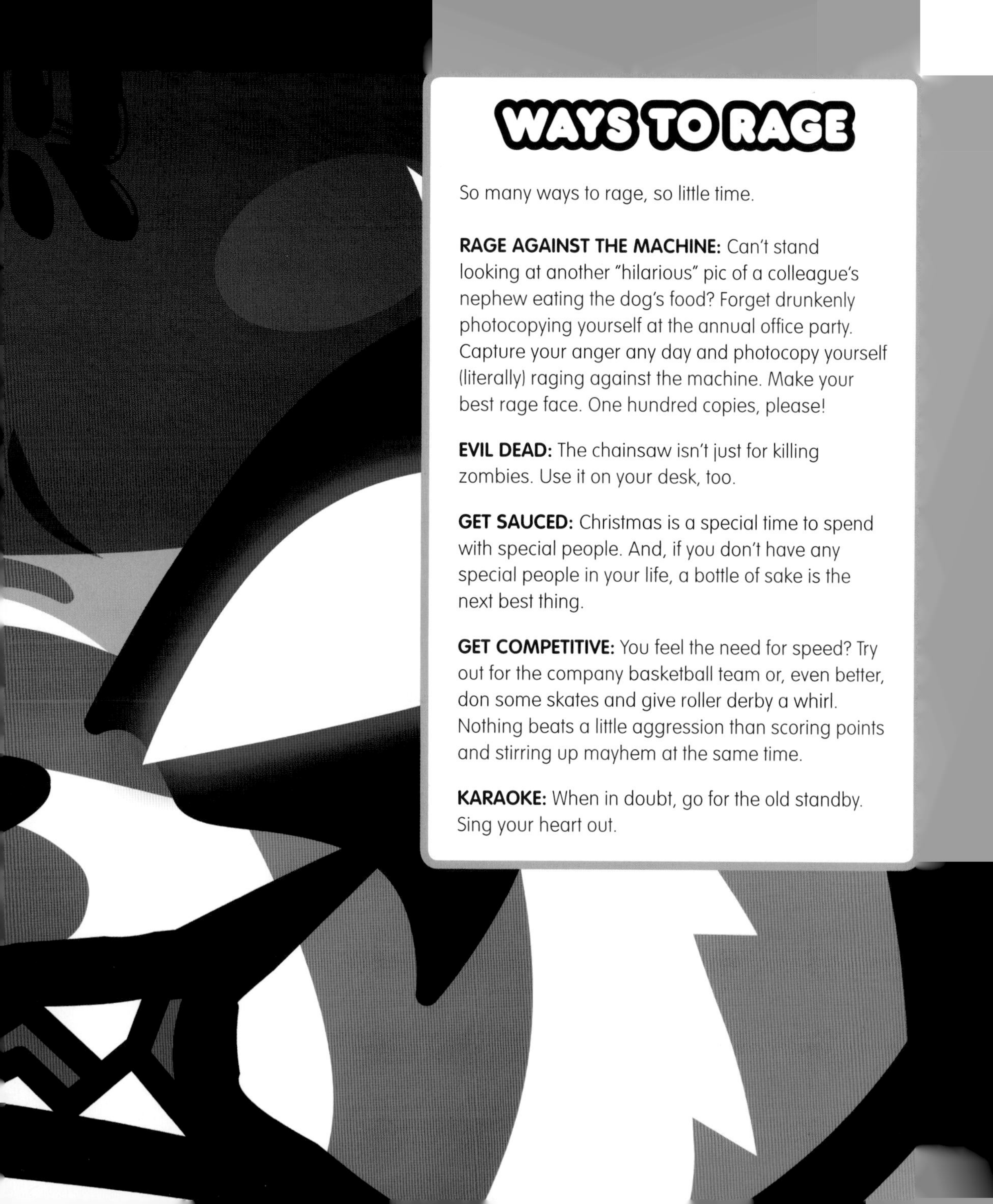

WAYS TO RAGE

So many ways to rage, so little time.

RAGE AGAINST THE MACHINE: Can't stand looking at another "hilarious" pic of a colleague's nephew eating the dog's food? Forget drunkenly photocopying yourself at the annual office party. Capture your anger any day and photocopy yourself (literally) raging against the machine. Make your best rage face. One hundred copies, please!

EVIL DEAD: The chainsaw isn't just for killing zombies. Use it on your desk, too.

GET SAUCED: Christmas is a special time to spend with special people. And, if you don't have any special people in your life, a bottle of sake is the next best thing.

GET COMPETITIVE: You feel the need for speed? Try out for the company basketball team or, even better, don some skates and give roller derby a whirl. Nothing beats a little aggression than scoring points and stirring up mayhem at the same time.

KARAOKE: When in doubt, go for the old standby. Sing your heart out.

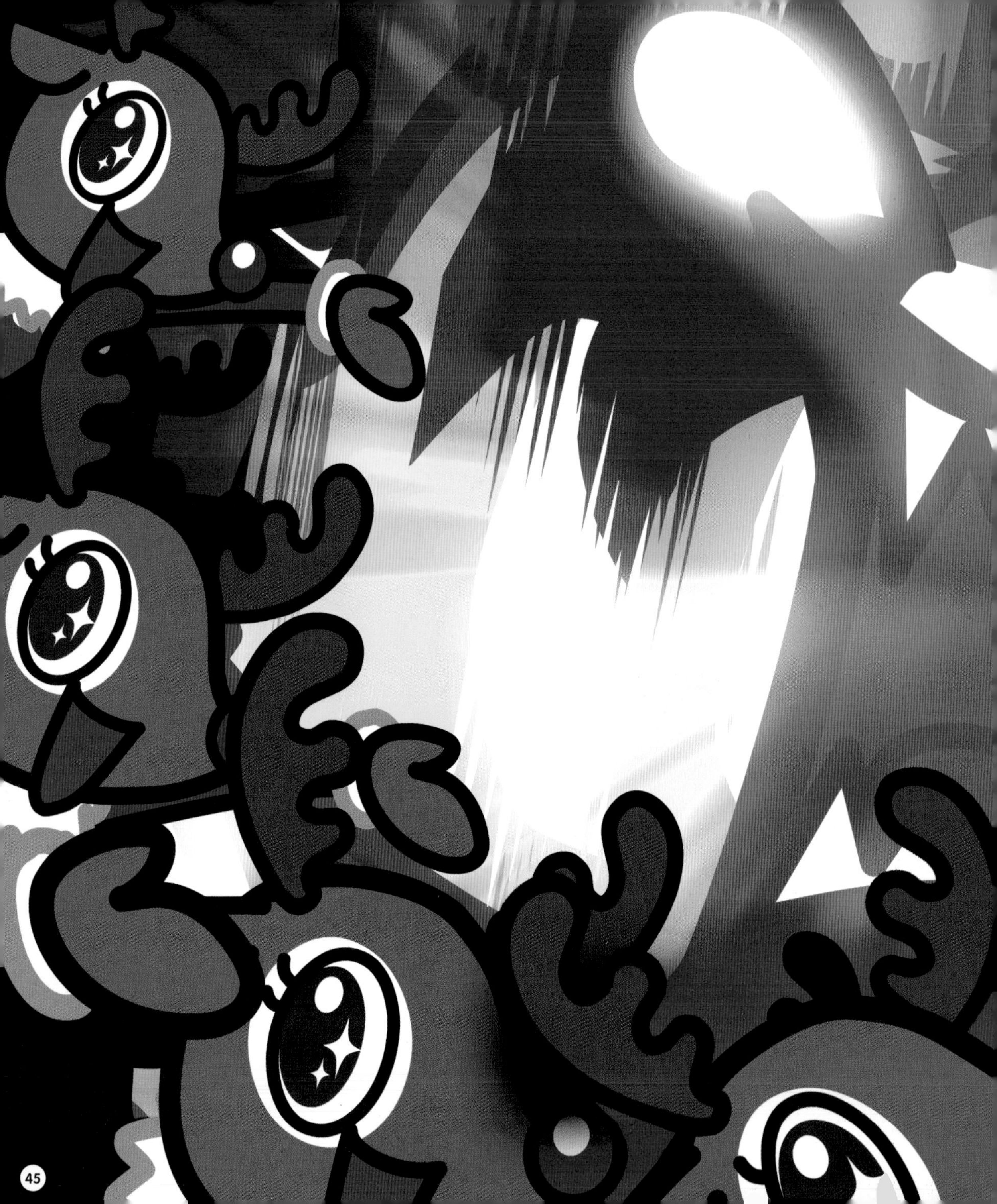

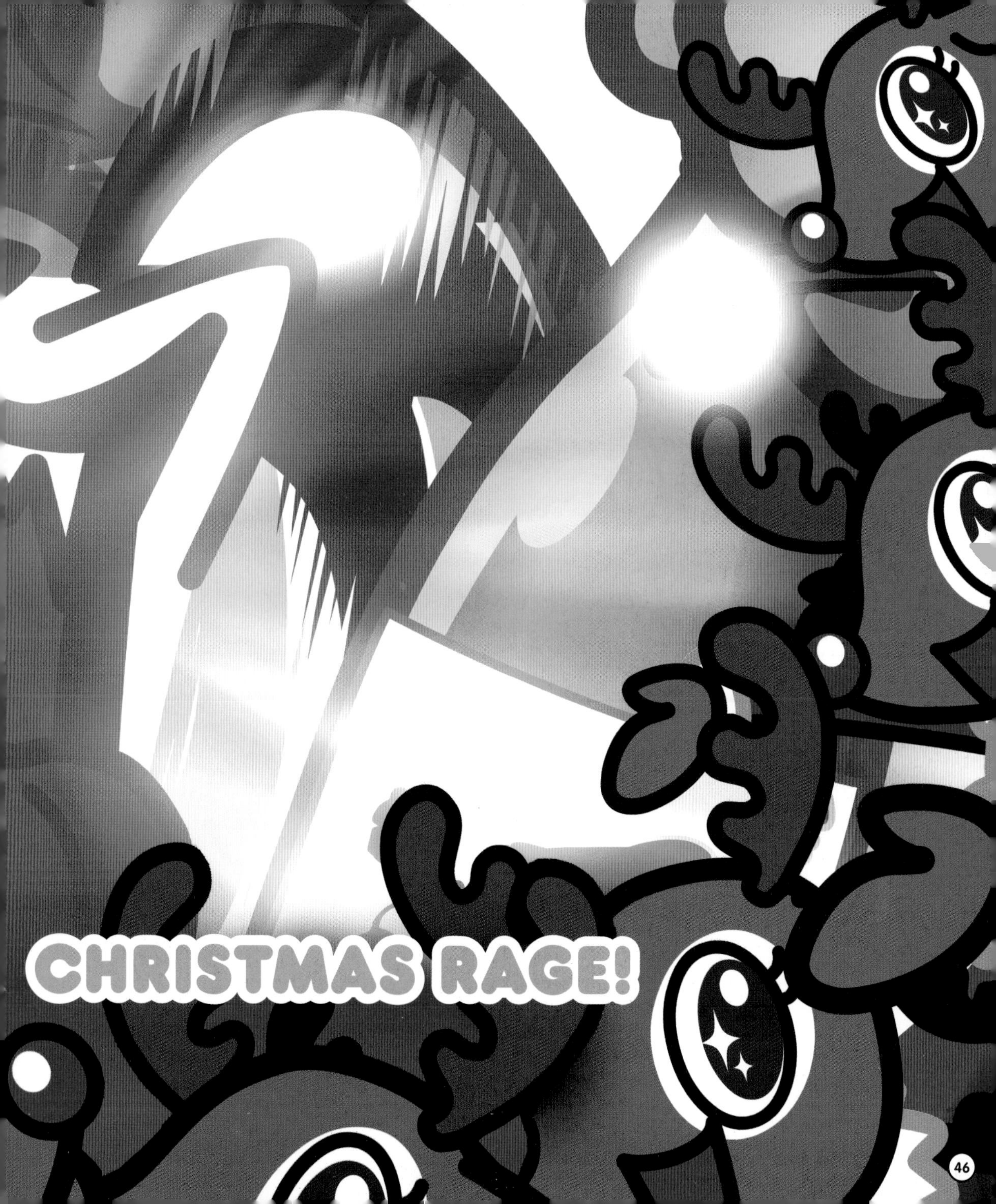

CHRISTMAS RAGE!

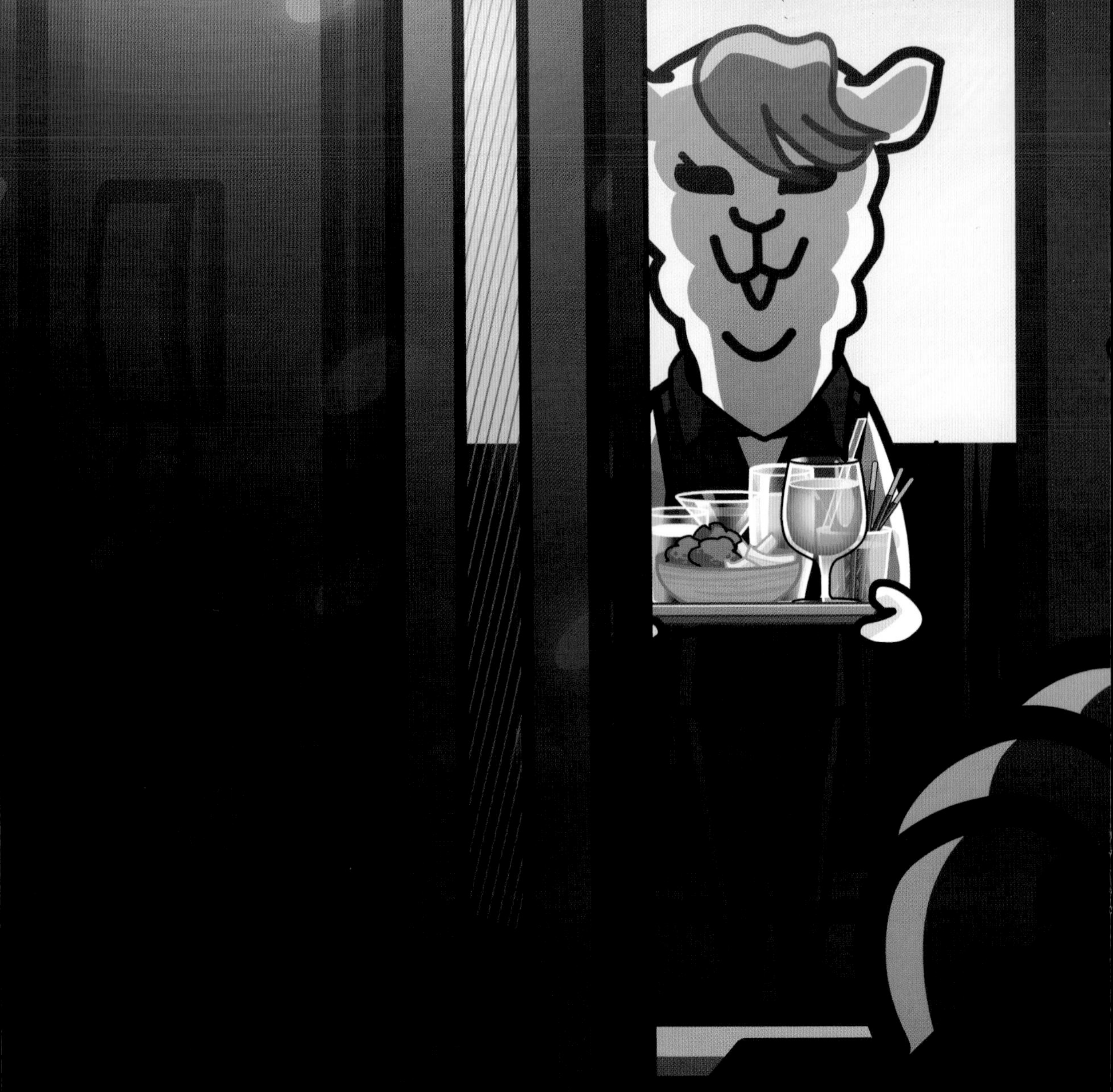

KARAOKE RAGE!

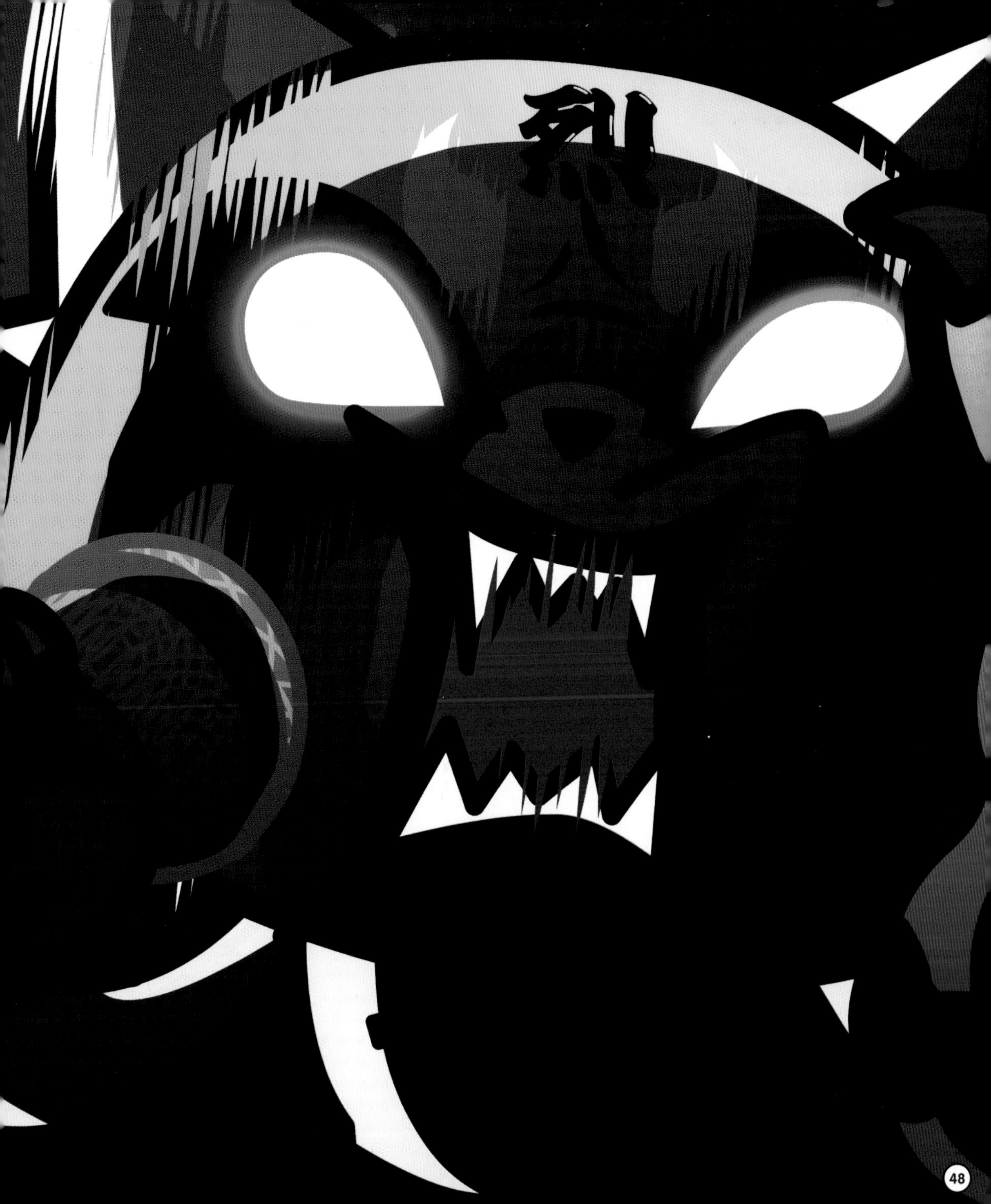
烈

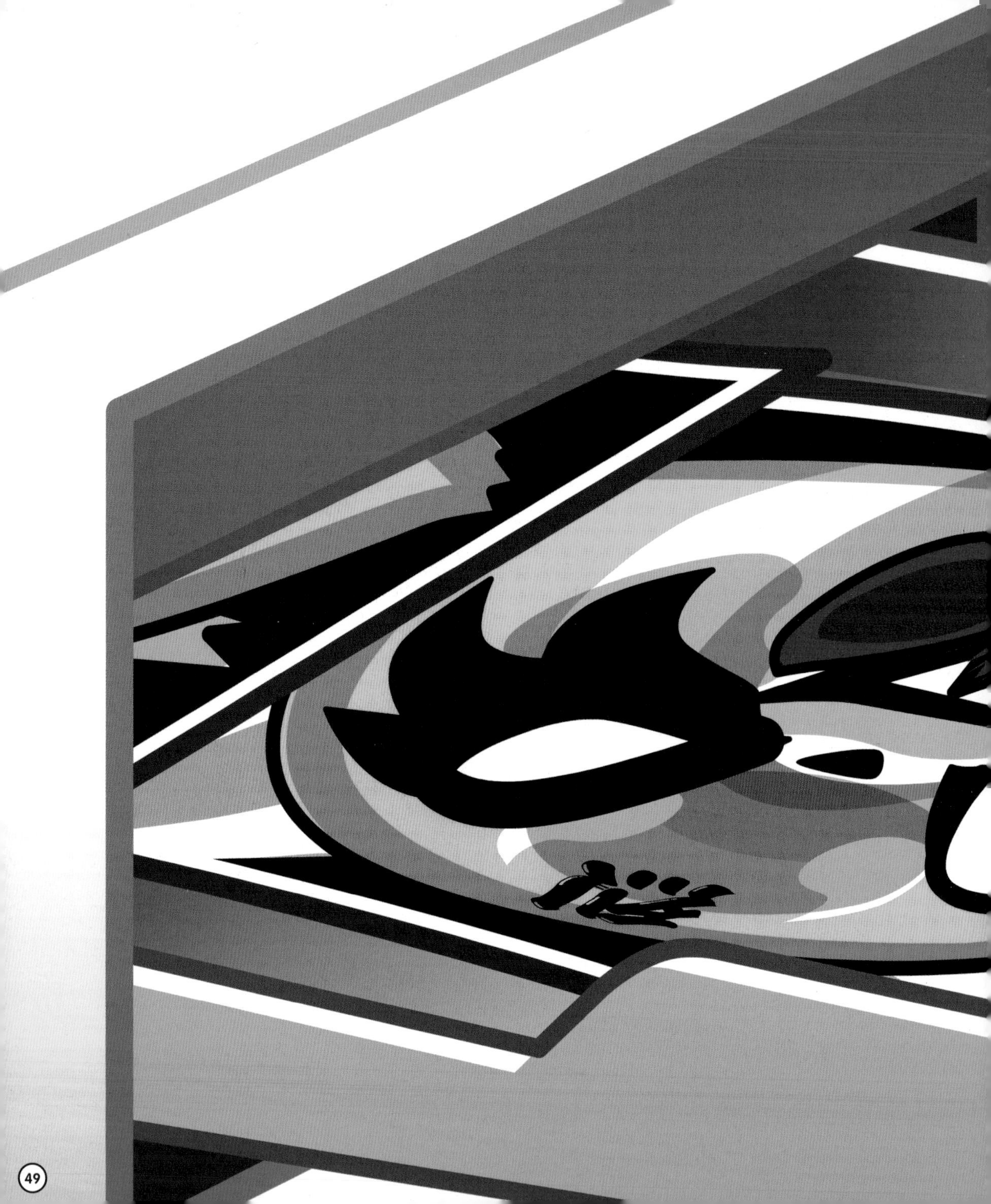

COPY MACHINE RAGE!

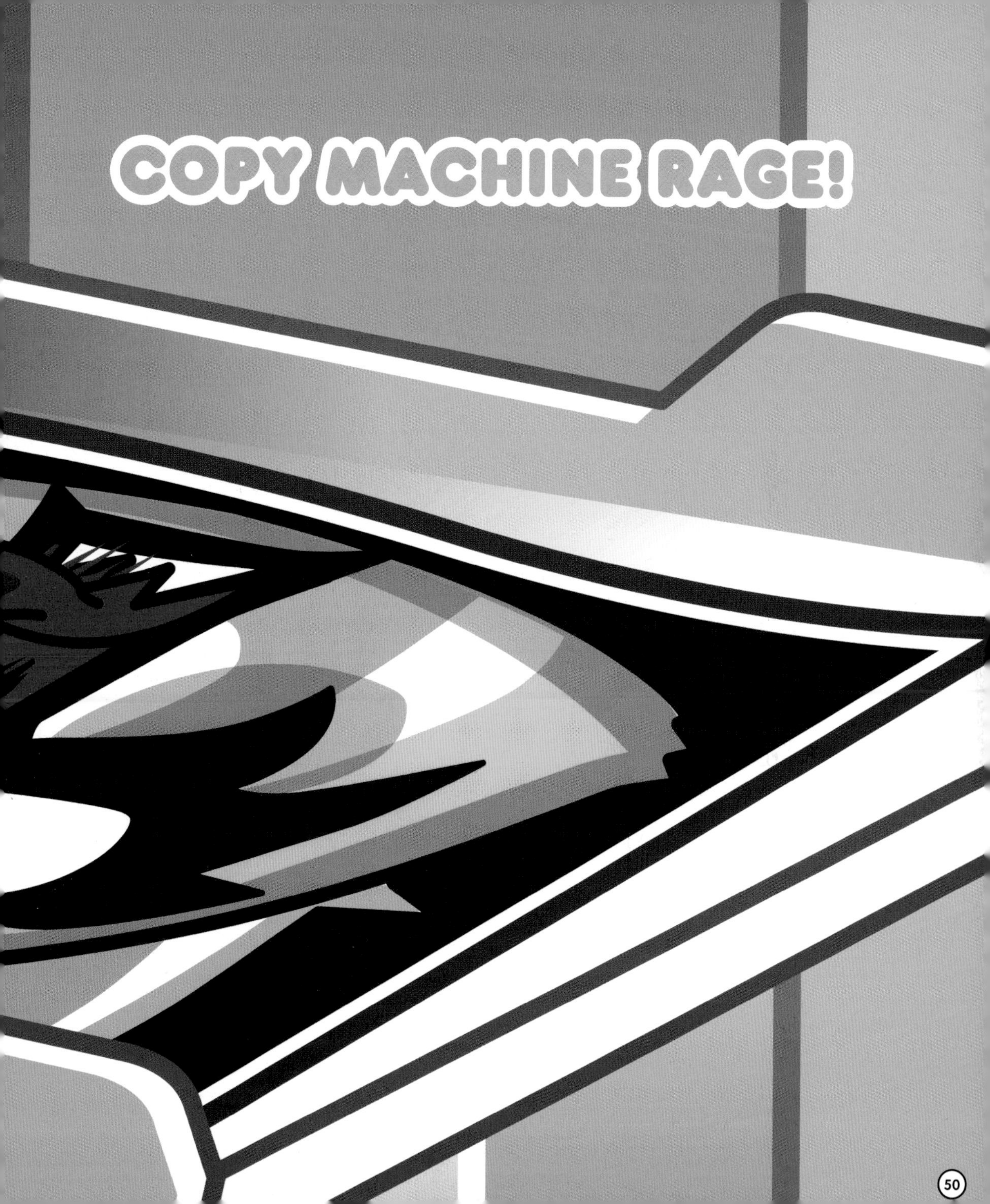

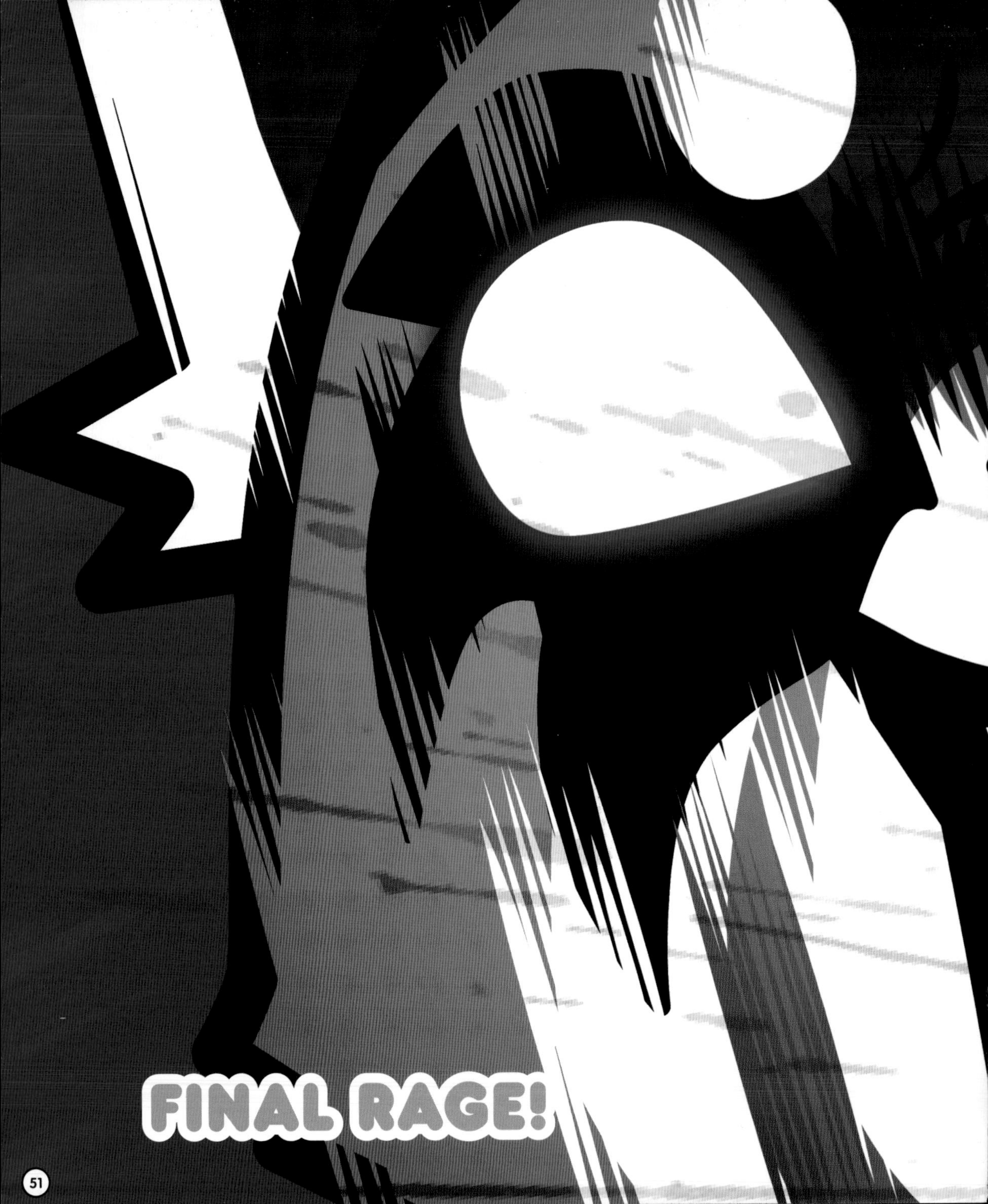
FINAL RAGE!

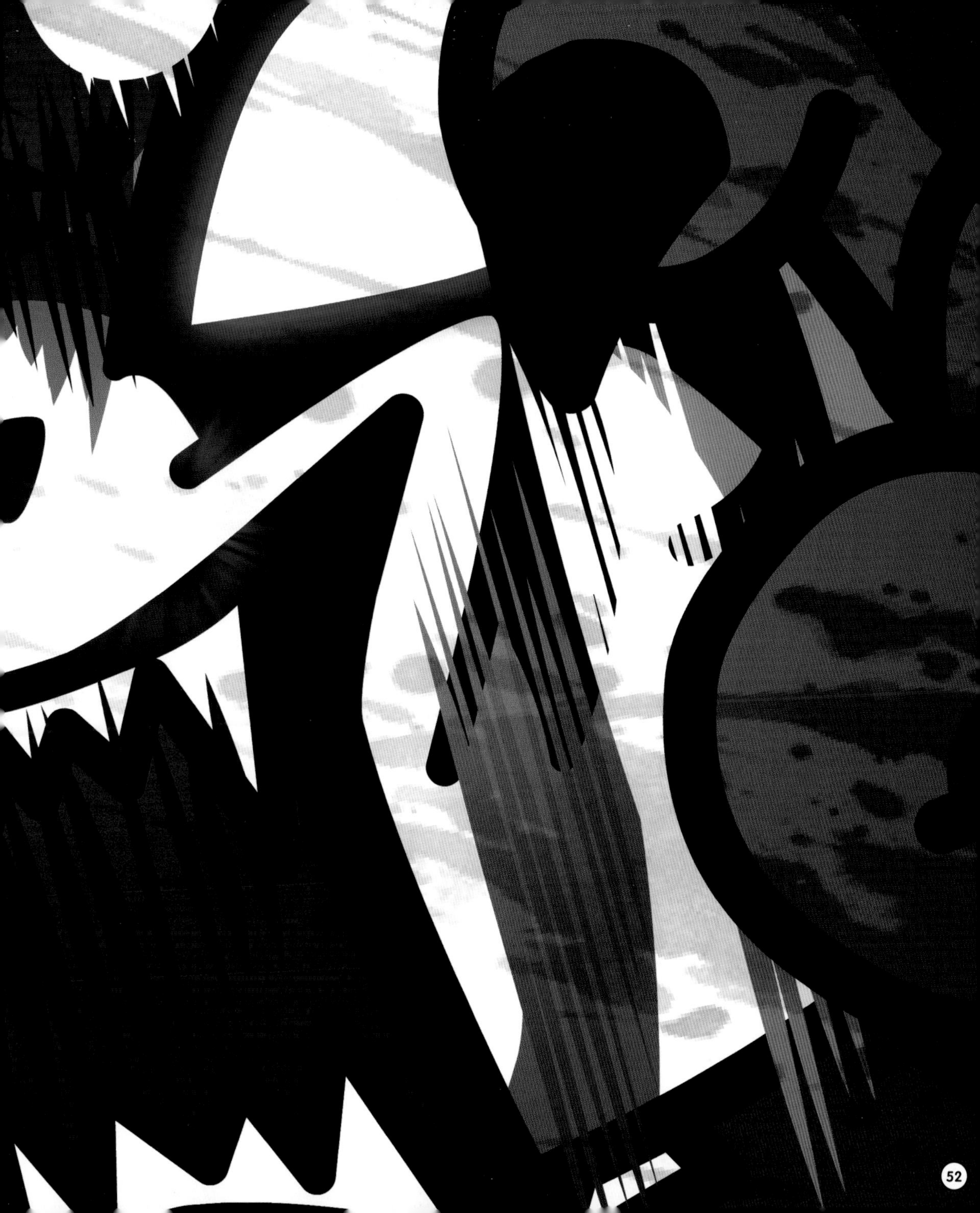

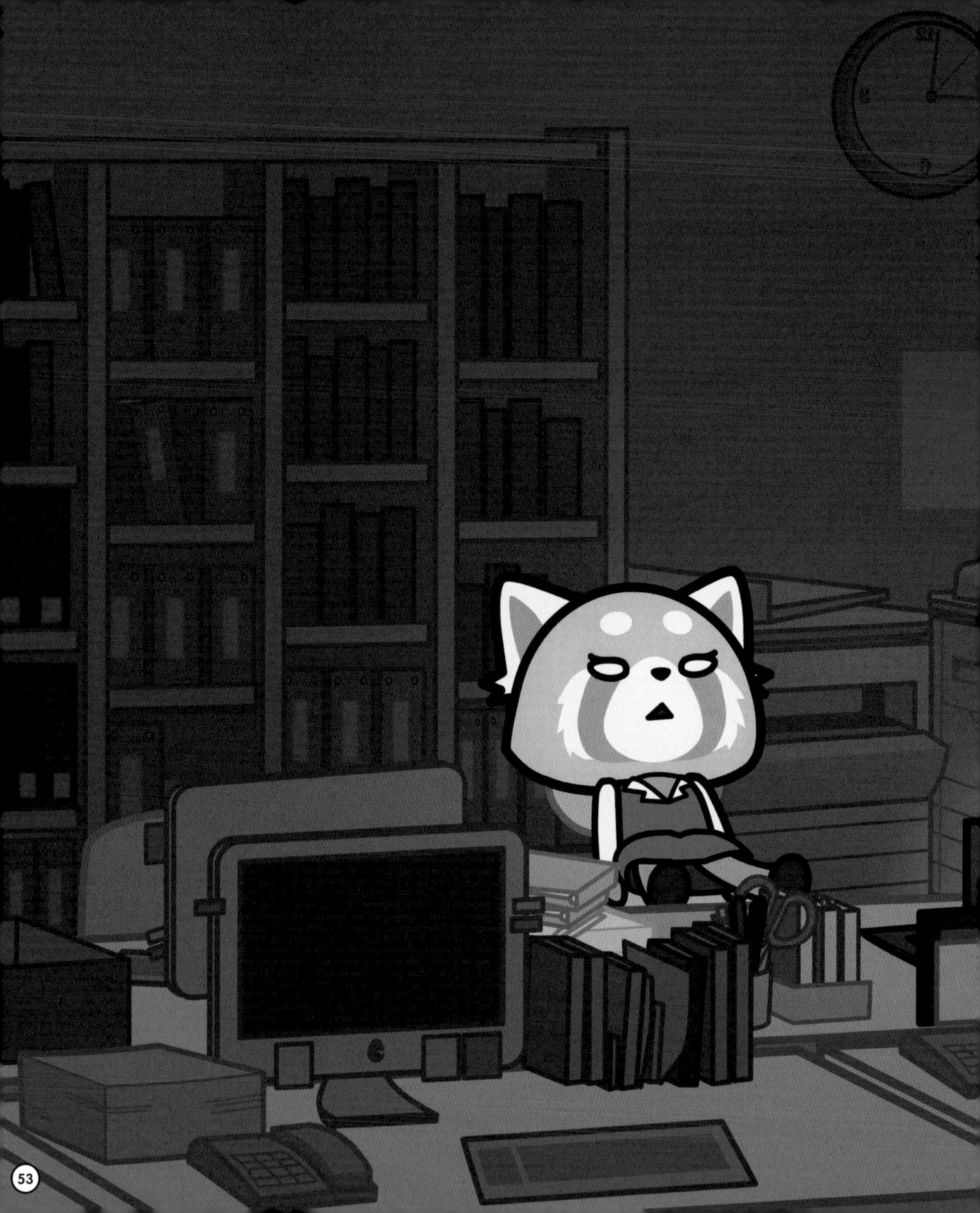

CHAPTER FOUR: WORKING LATE

The only thing worse than waking up early is staying late at the office, a routine I'm sadly very familiar with. Sure, you could waltz out the door at 5 PM and head to the local watering hole, or you could stay behind, put in another few hours on the annual report, order dinner, and watch the moon rise over your colleagues' cubicle walls. It's not bad to put in a little extra work every once in awhile, especially when you can get more stuff done without your co-workers' constant chit-chat or the back-to-back meetings that eat up most days. There are other benefits that come from working late, too: you beat the after-work commuting crowd, and the best parties start late.

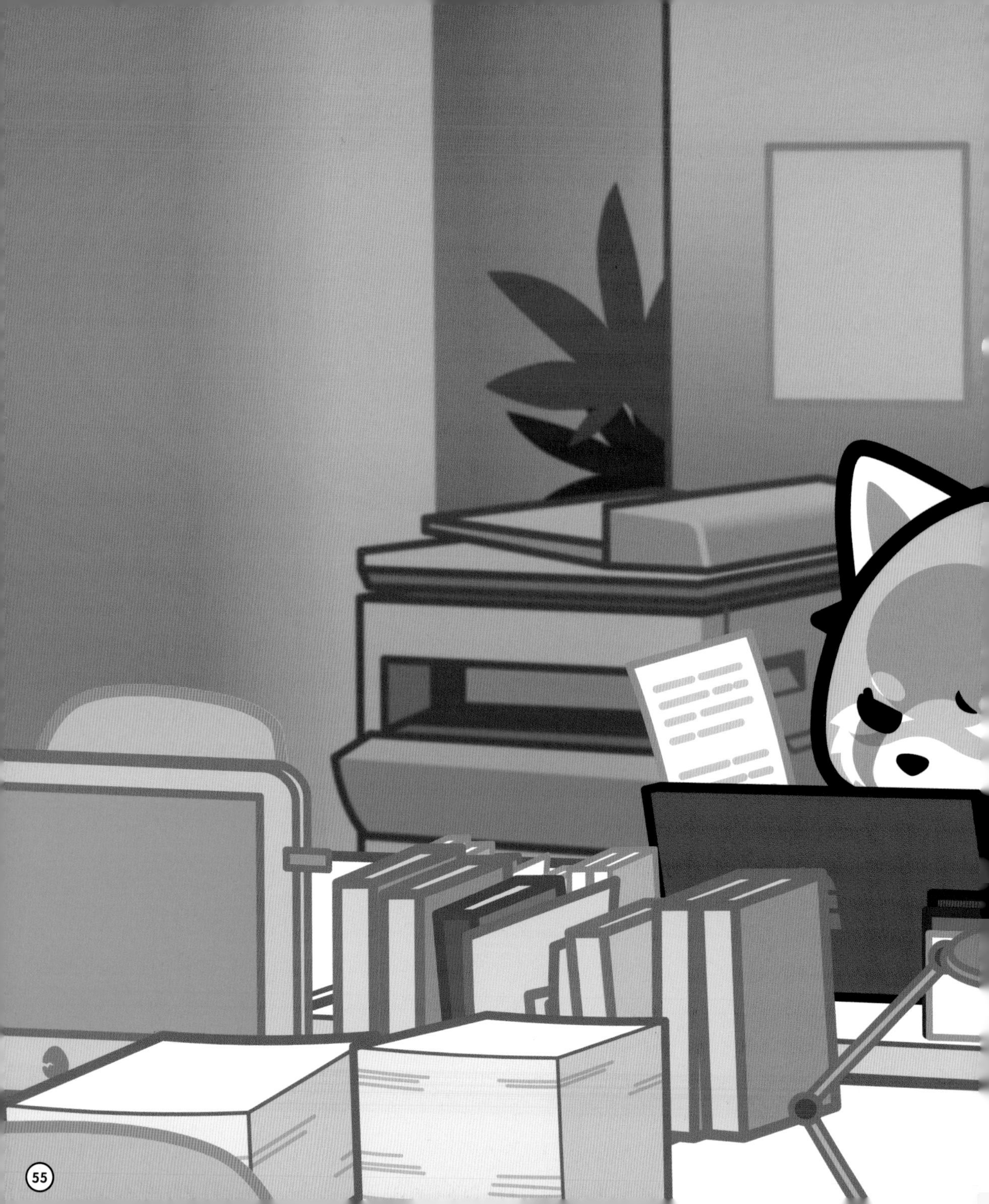

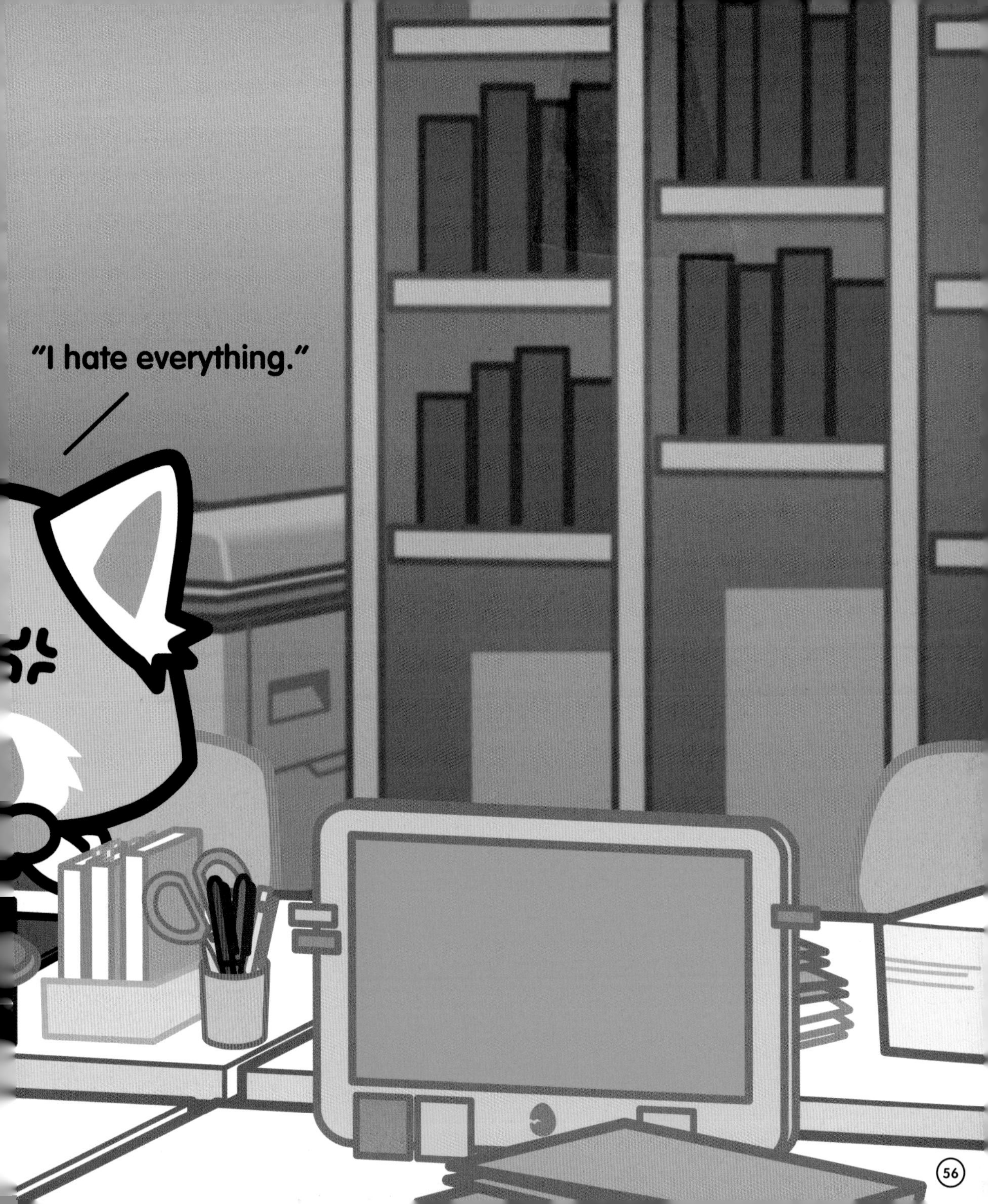
"I hate everything."

HOW TO PASS TIME WORKING LATE

Staying late affords certain . . . freedoms. And on really late-night workdays, when getting to the bar afterwards seems impossible and you feel like a slave to your job, it's important to claim some fun wherever you can find it. If that means spinning in your office chair with wild abandon until your boss finds you in the thralls of self-enjoyment, so be it. If he asks if you're having fun, your face should say it all (before you fall out of the chair and do a face plant): rage on.

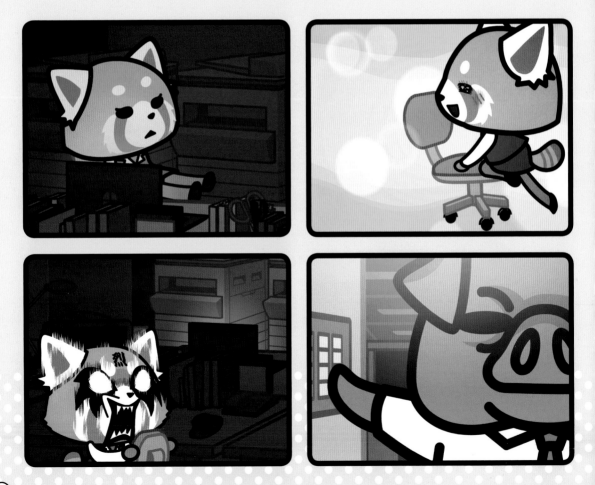

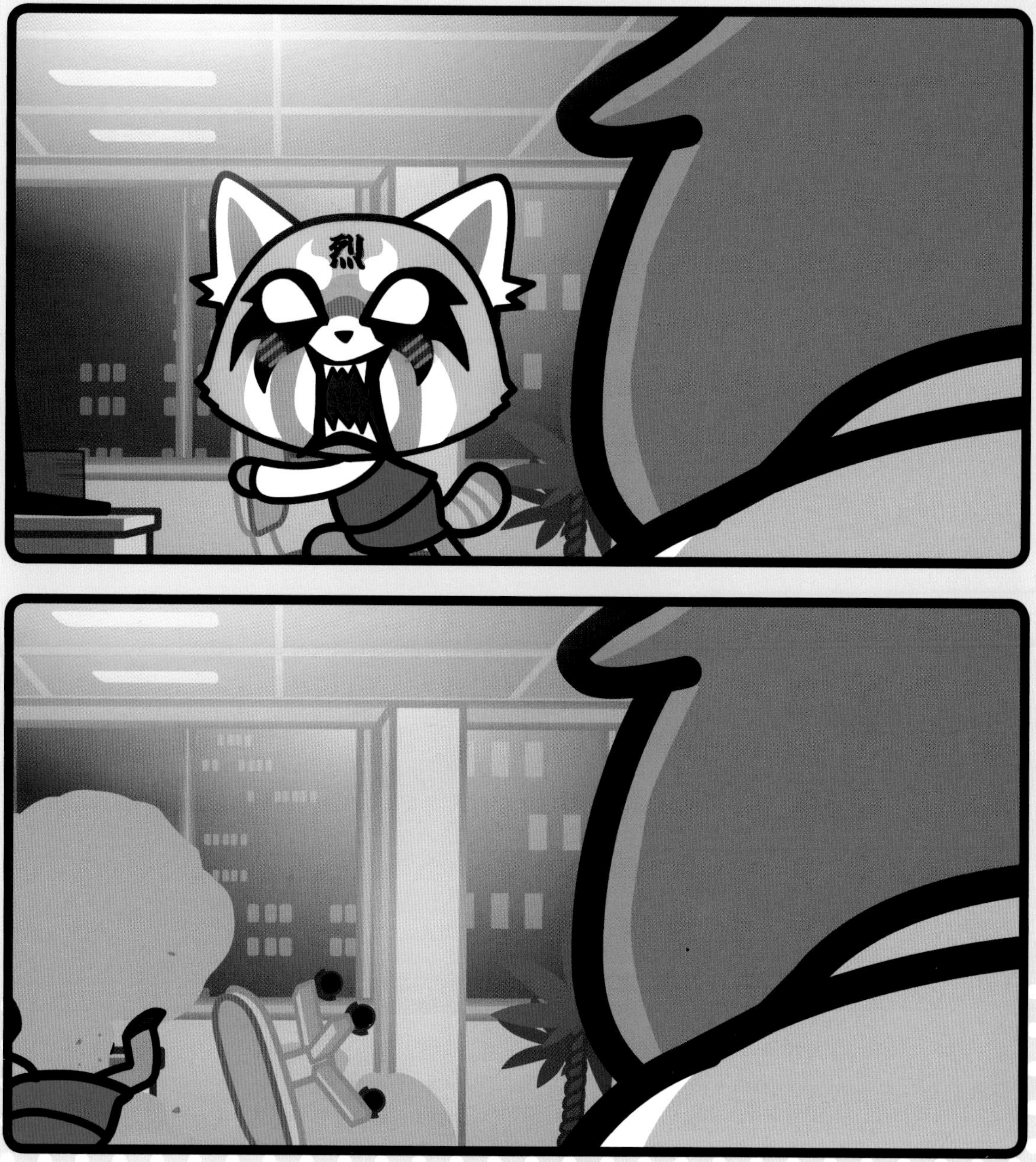
烈

WORKING LATE MEANS THIS IS YOUR NIGHT LIFE:

EAT

BATHE

BRUSH

SLEEP

TIP

To avoid a repetitive cycle where life becomes meaningless and you lose all hope while falling into a pit of despair created by soul-sucking office jobs, make sure to take frequent breaks, set aside time to see friends (NOT colleagues) outside of work, take up a hobby, and remember who you are.

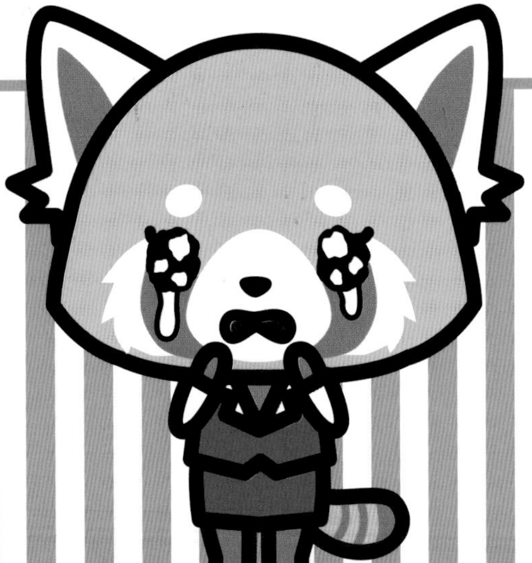

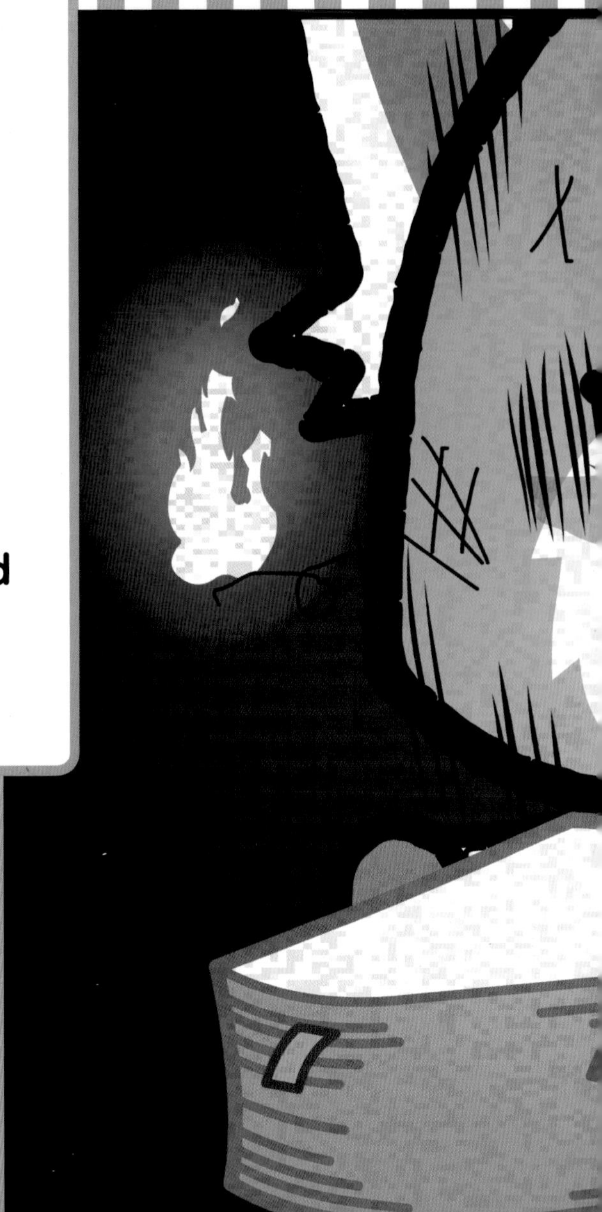

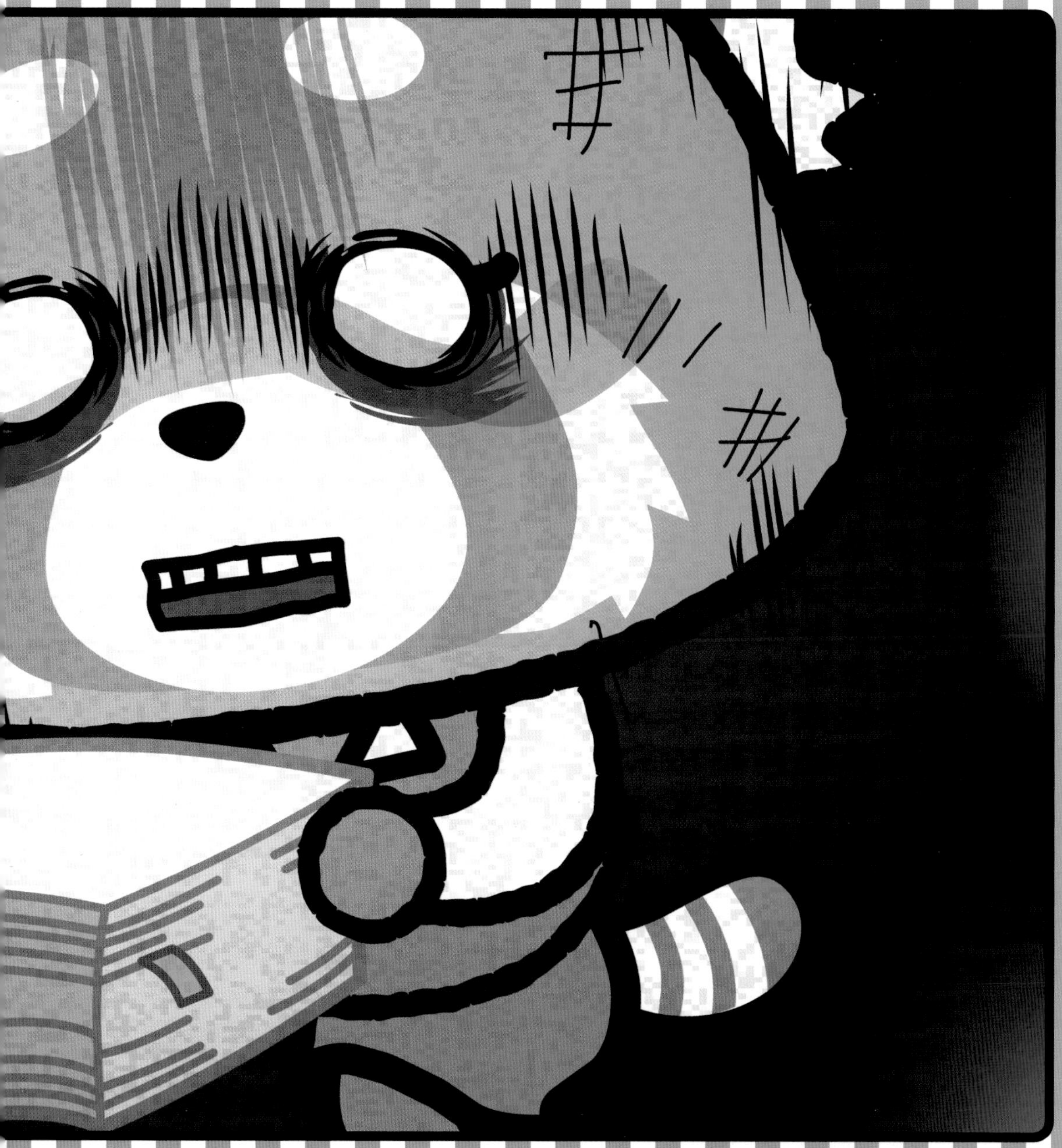

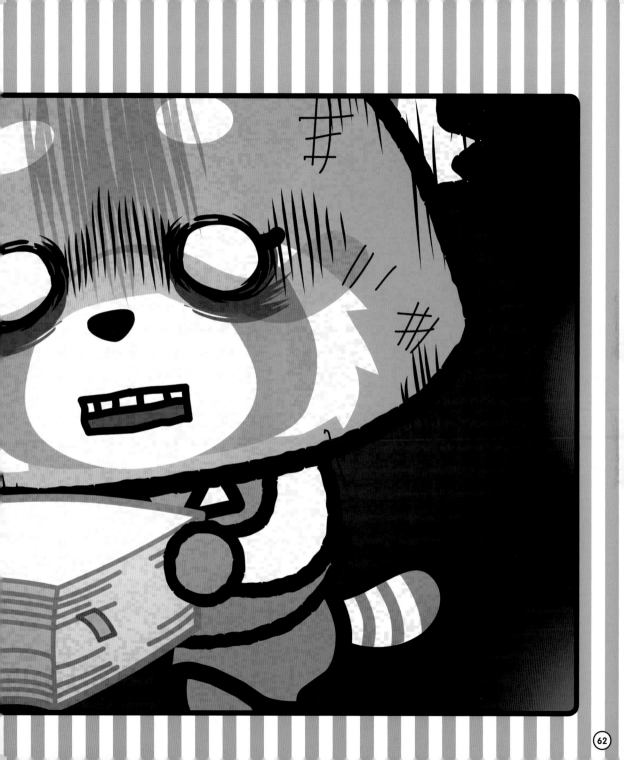

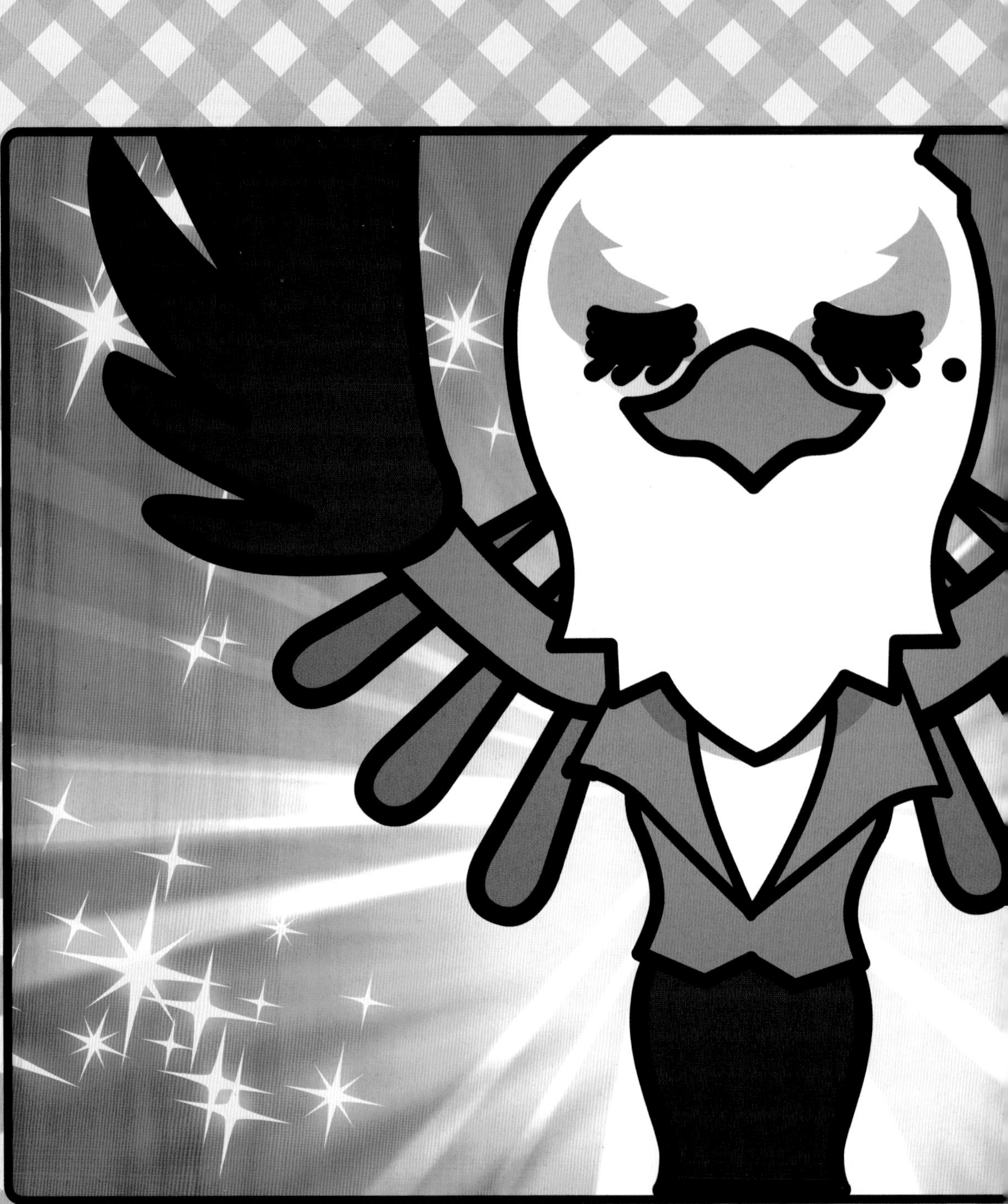

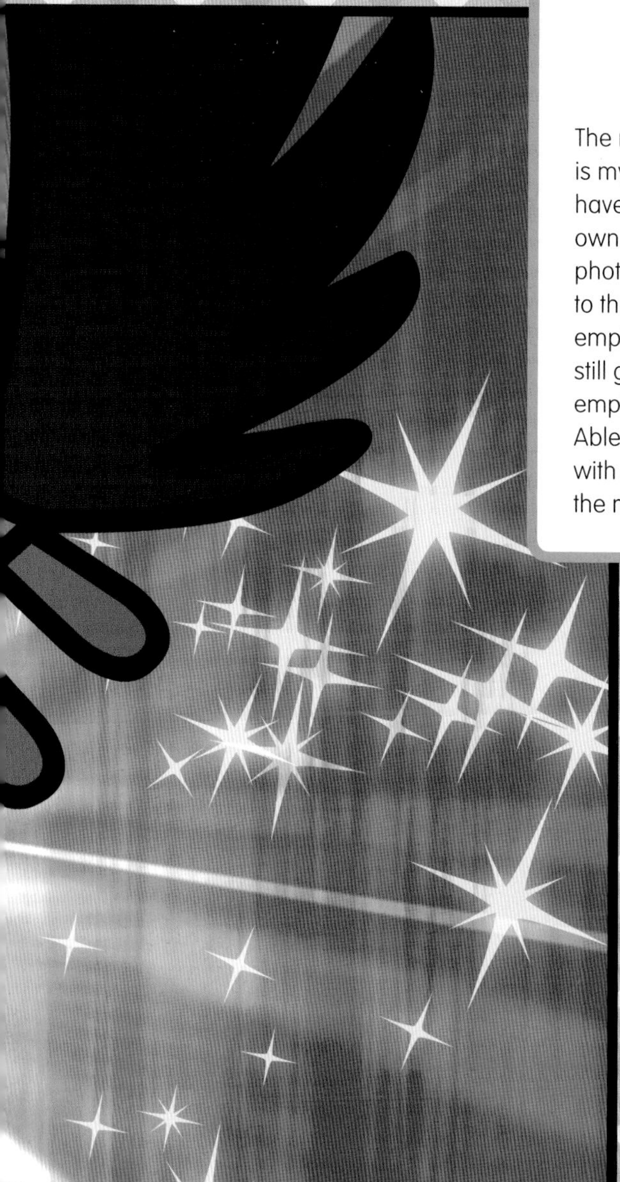

THE MODEL EMPLOYEE

The model employee—cool, calm, and poised—is my virtual opposite, which is not to say I don't have certain strengths or "model" behavior of my own. (I happen to be excellent, for example, at photocopying.) In my office, Washimi is the secretary to the president and the very definition of the model employee. Despite her unflappable presence, she still gristles at the way her boss treats her fellow employees, which makes her A-OK in my book. Able to balance the professional and the personal with ease, I can only say one thing about Washimi, the model employee: watch and learn.

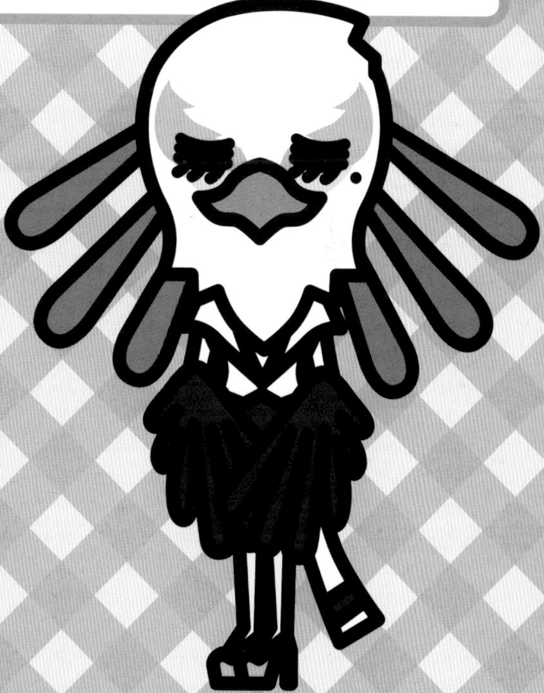

CHECKING WORK EMAIL AT HOME

A Cautionary Tale

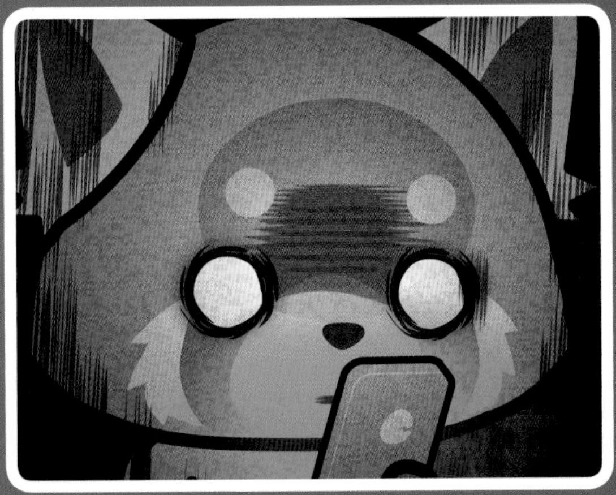

It's impossible to resist

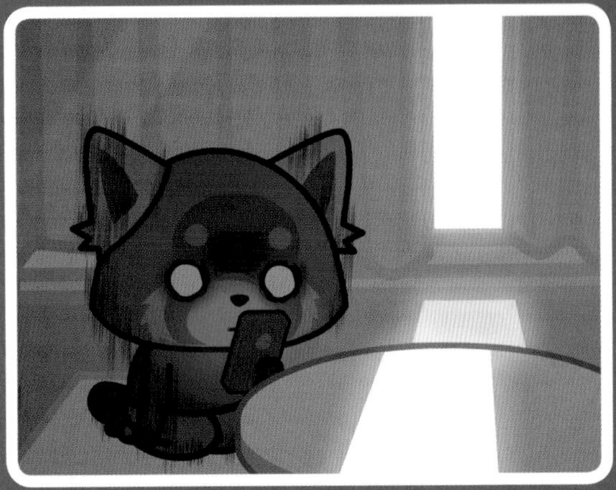

But don't let it take over

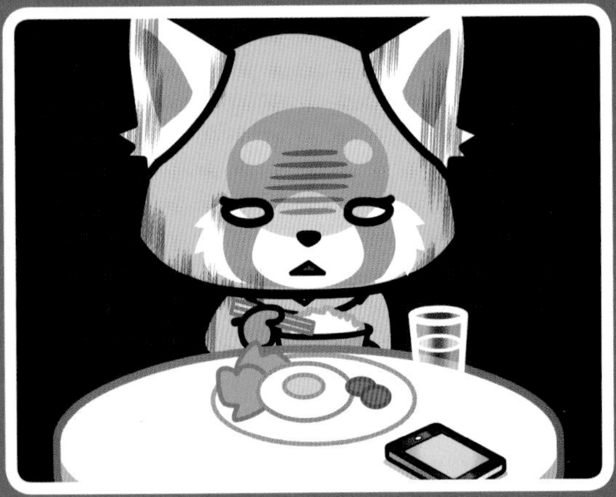

Do NOT bring it to the table

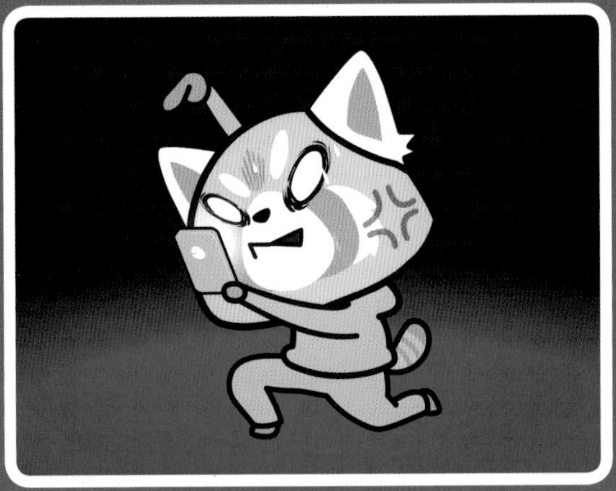

DO NOT CHECK YOUR EMAIL IN YOUR PAJAMAS

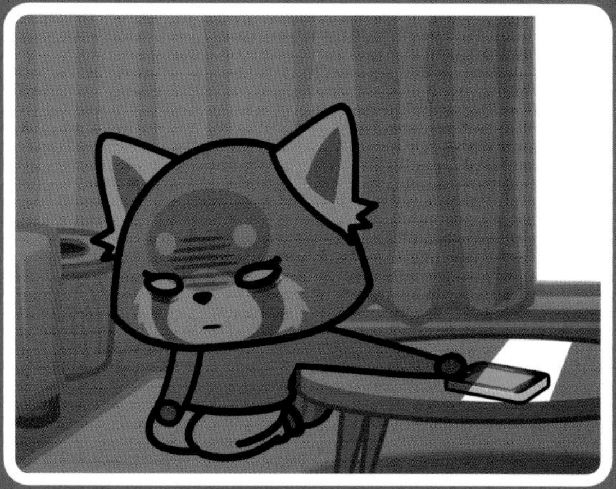

Just put your phone down

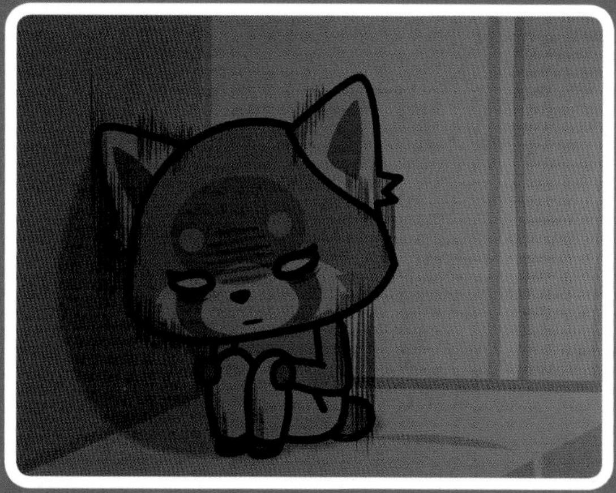

Try to ignore it

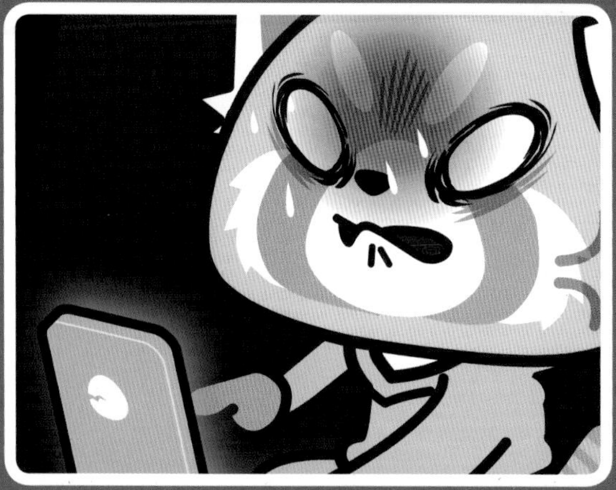

WORK RAGE BELONGS AT WORK

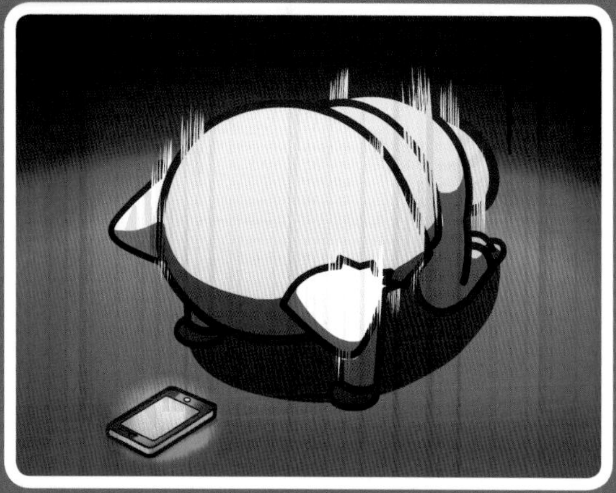

TEAR YOURSELF AWAY

PASSING THE BUCK

Oh, and if a colleague asks you to help her out with something because she has to leave early, do not trust her. I trusted someone once and it did not end well.

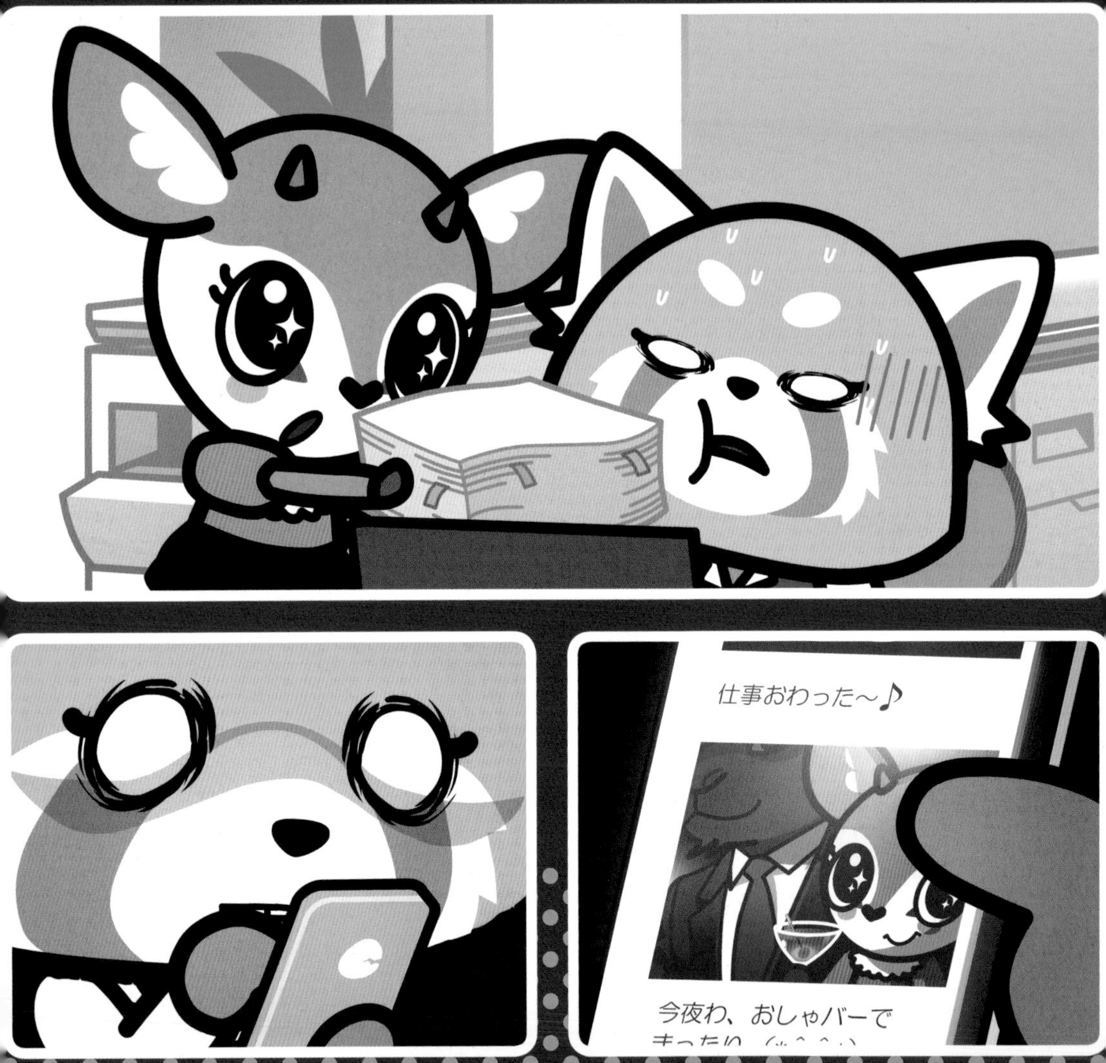

仕事おわった〜♪
今夜わ、おしゃバーで

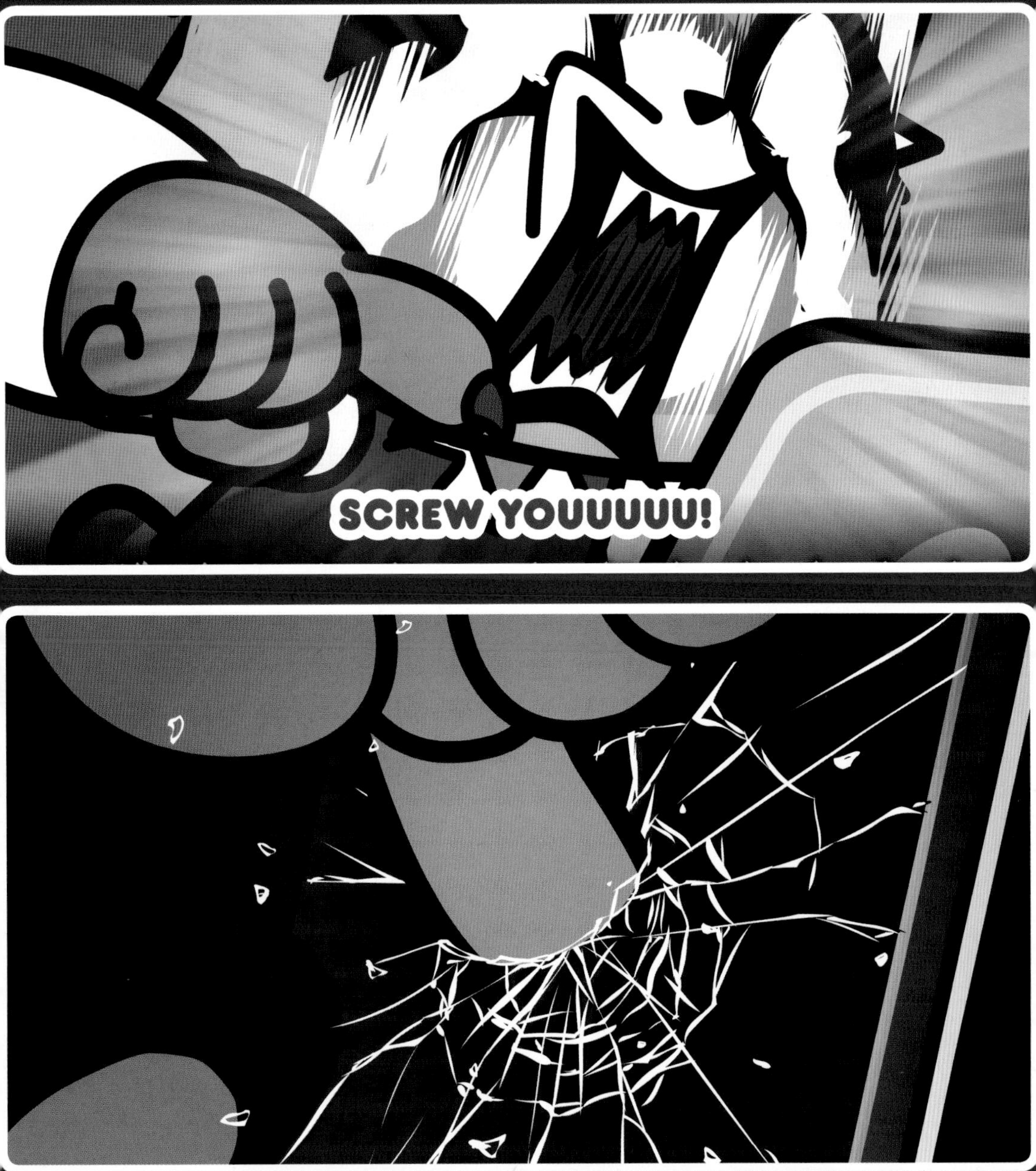
SCREW YOUUUUU!

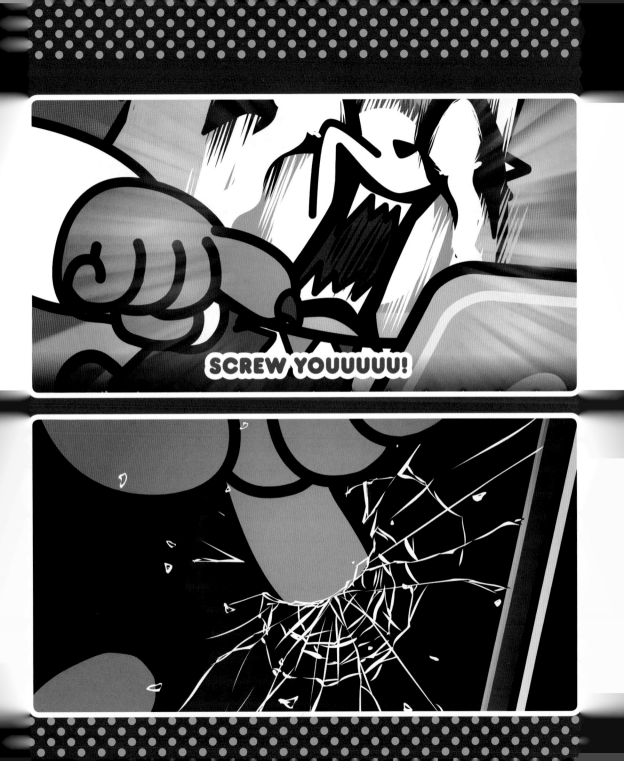

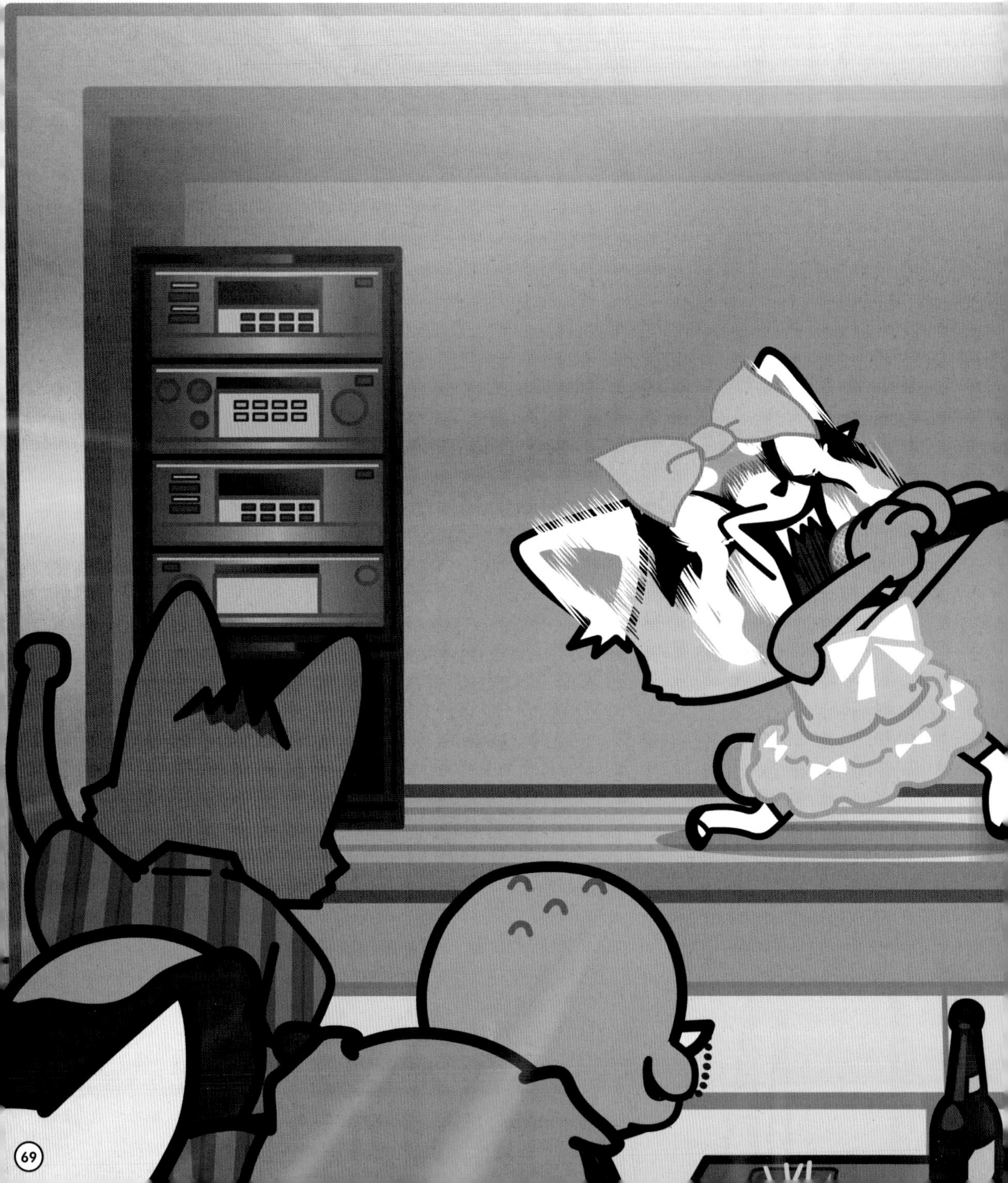

CHAPTER FIVE: WORK HARD, PARTY HARDER!

The trick to working hard is to party hard, too. Sometimes, it's the only way to successfully balance the stress. Massages and yoga are good, but beer is cheaper, and there's nothing better—and more stress-relieving—than to sing-scream a few lines of karaoke into a dimly lit room with people cheering you on. Sure, you may regret that last drink or the one after that tomorrow. Until then, though, live like it's your last. Go for the high note. Say "yes" to adventures—even if they happen at midnight. You know where you're going to be Monday to Friday, 9 AM till 5 PM (if not longer): so why not live a little outside the cubicle? The secret to not overdoing it is to check in with yourself. If you need to, refer back to the Top Ten Things to Remember at Happy Hour (see page 78), and if you can't successfully (or honestly) answer those questions, it's time to straighten up and fly right.

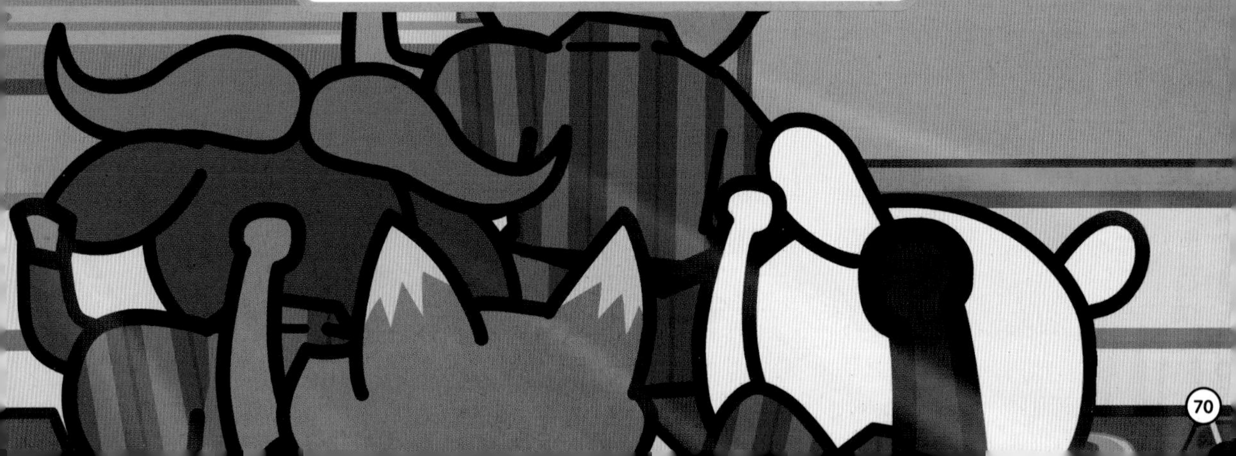

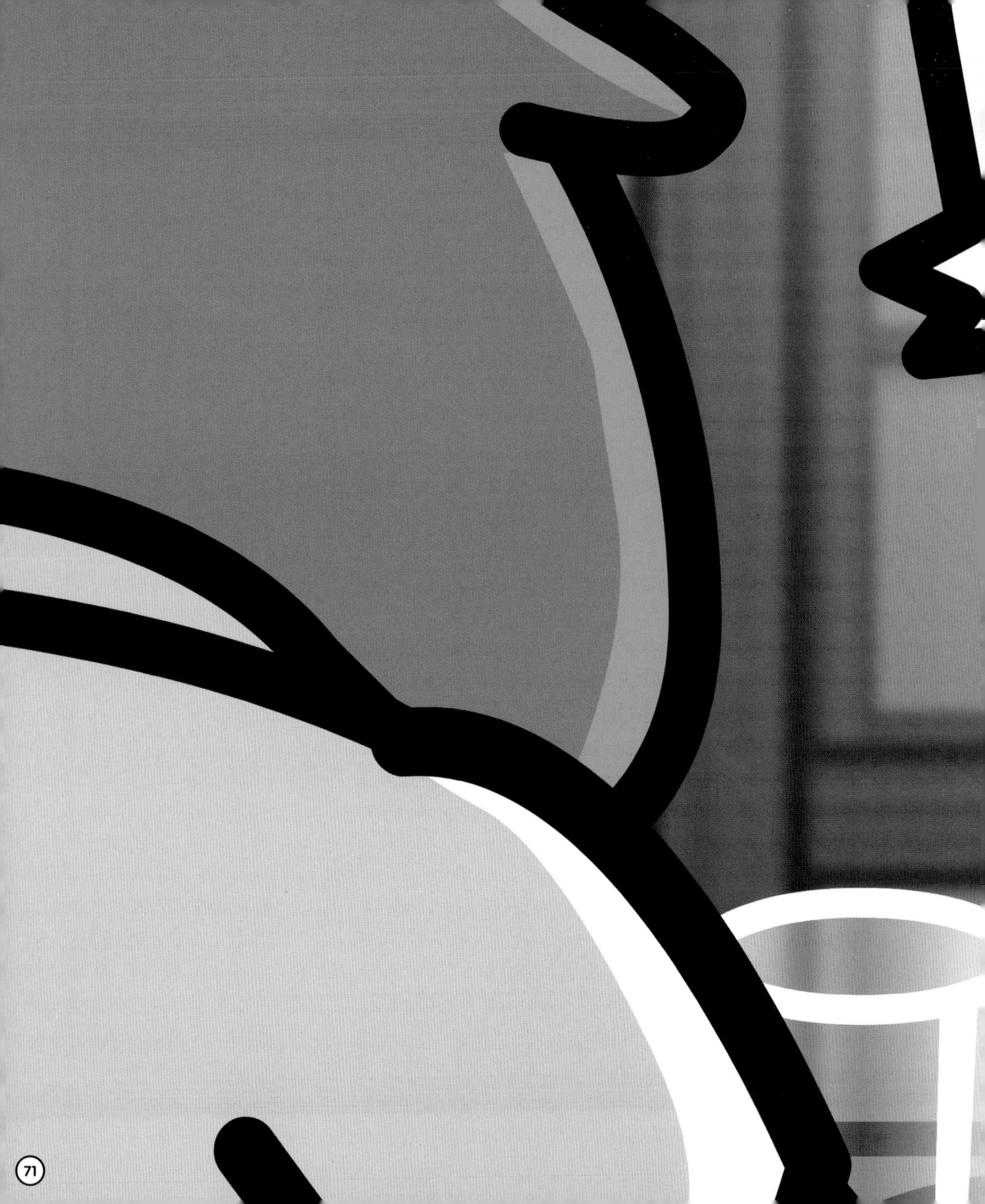

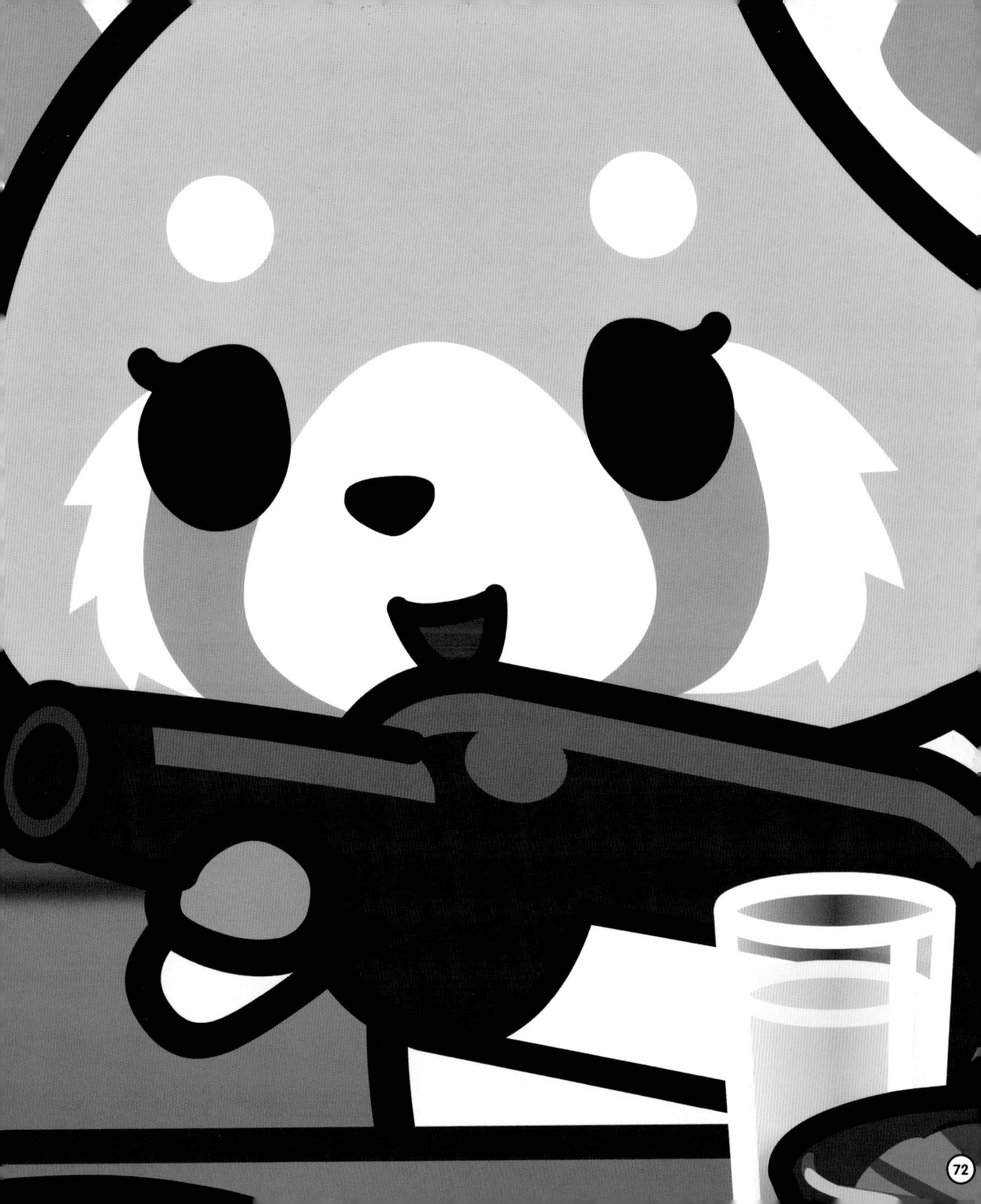

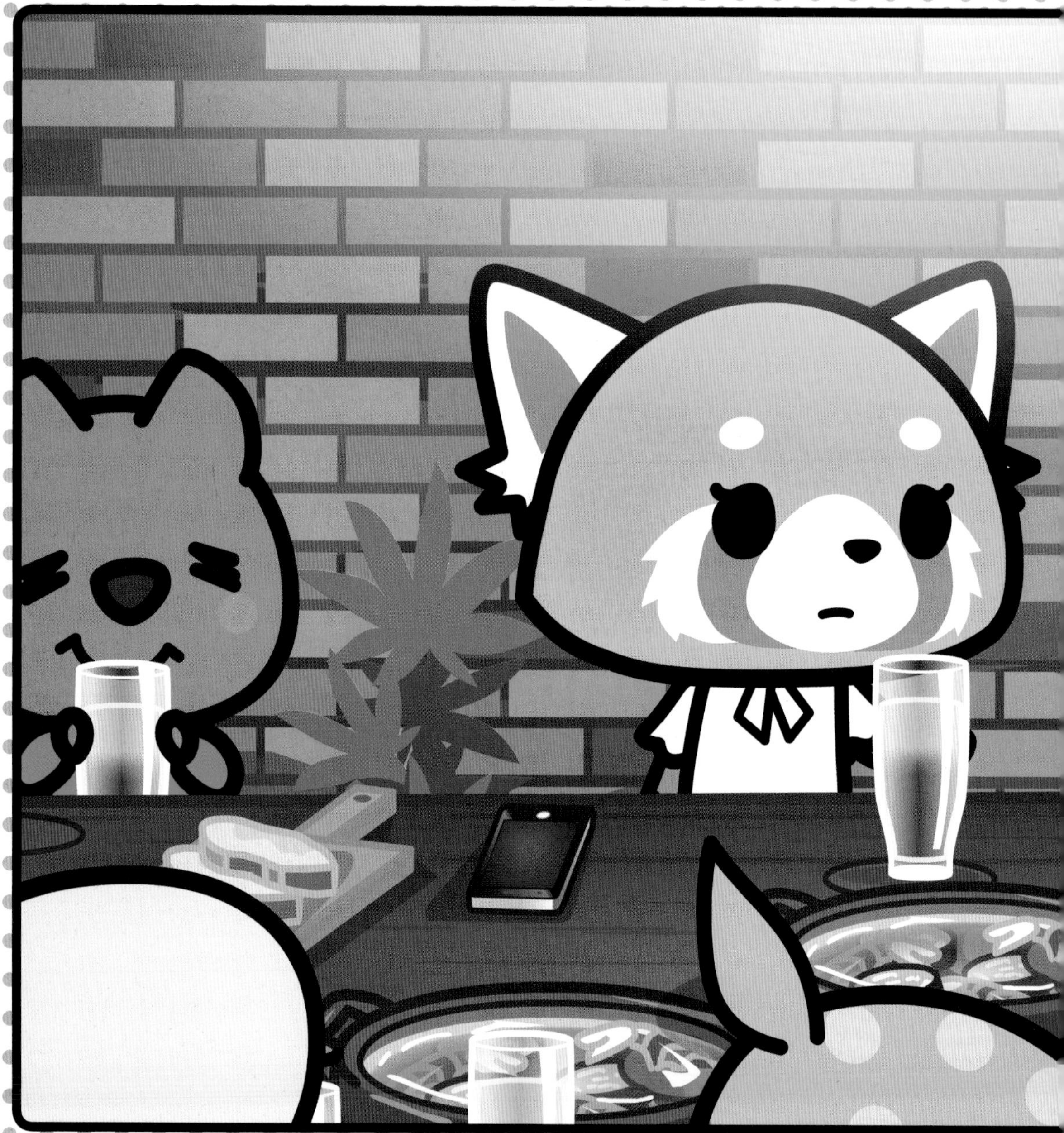

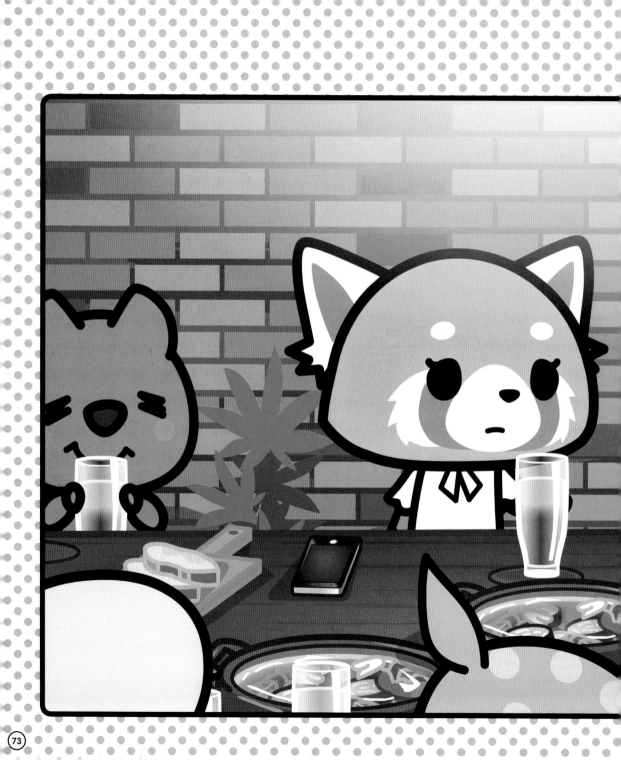

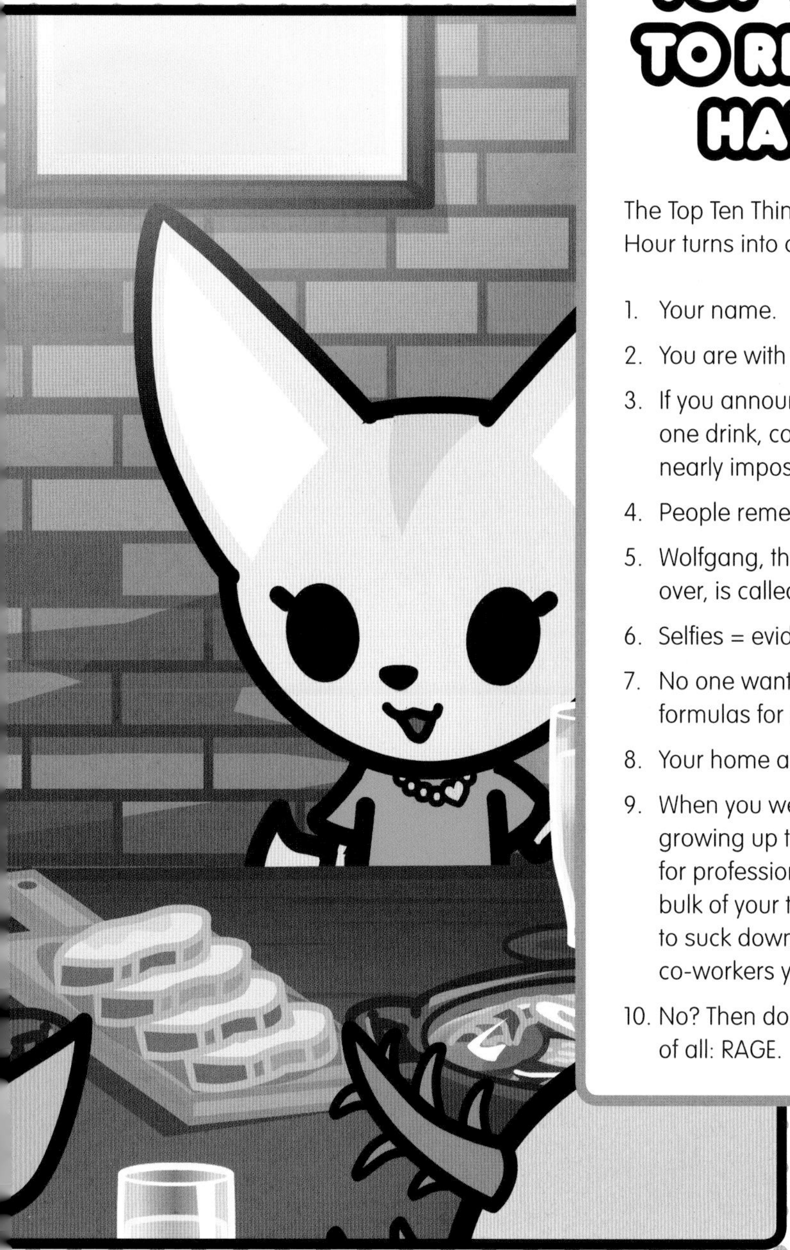

TOP TEN THINGS TO REMEMBER AT HAPPY HOUR

The Top Ten Things to Remember *before* Happy Hour turns into a Happy All-Nighter:

1. Your name.
2. You are with your colleagues.
3. If you announce that you're just going to have one drink, commit to it. Just kidding, I know that's nearly impossible.
4. People remember embarrassing stories.
5. Wolfgang, the sexy accountant three cubicles over, is called "Wolf" for good reason.
6. Selfies = evidence.
7. No one wants to hear a story about cheat sheet formulas for Excel.
8. Your home address.
9. When you were a little girl, did you dream about growing up to have a menial job with little hope for professional advancement and to spend the bulk of your twenties using your college degree to suck down three-for-one drink specials with co-workers you barely tolerate?
10. No? Then don't forget the most important thing of all: RAGE.

THE LOUD AND TALKATIVE OVERSHARER

Every office has one: the loud and talkative oversharer. Kabae, the office assistant next to me, doesn't get it: with her booming voice, she makes sure I hear every detail of her rambling conversations. It doesn't matter who she's speaking to—her nephew, her sister, the janitor, our boss, the mailman, herself—I hear it all. Being surrounded by such a large personality inevitably may make you feel small, but you're not. You're a strong and mighty red panda and the next time your oversharer wants to show you another family photograph or tell you about her weekend shopping trip, silently repeat these three words until they tumble from your mouth with the confidence of a big-arena rock star: "No, thank you!"

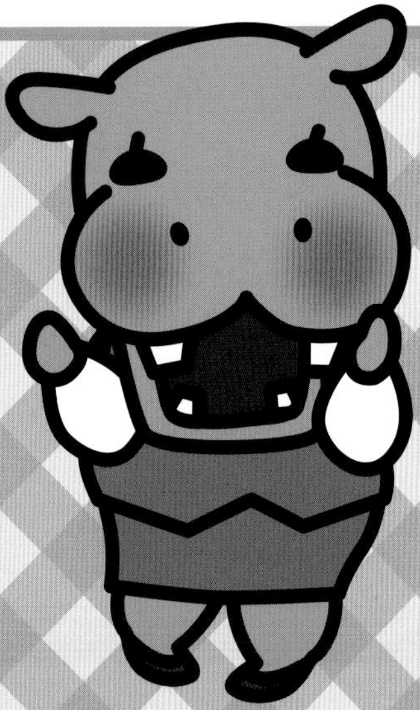

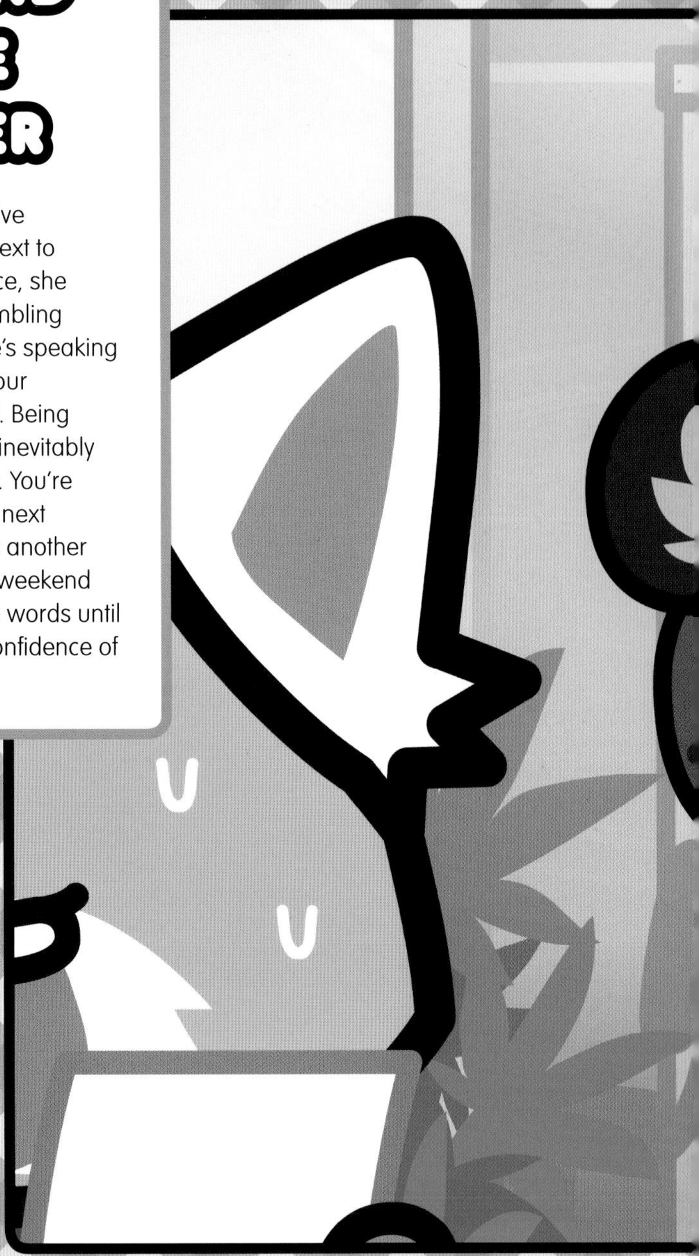

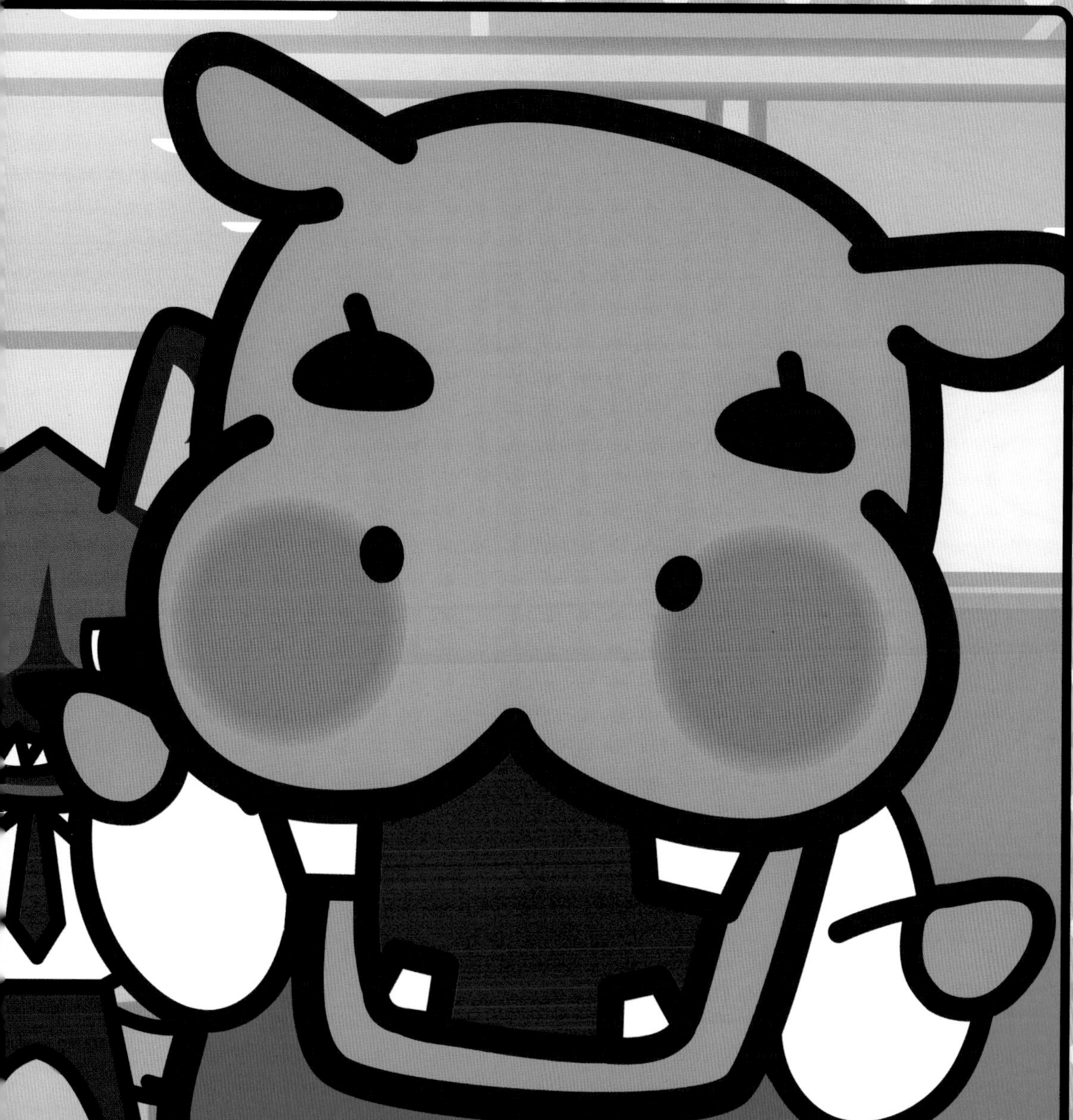

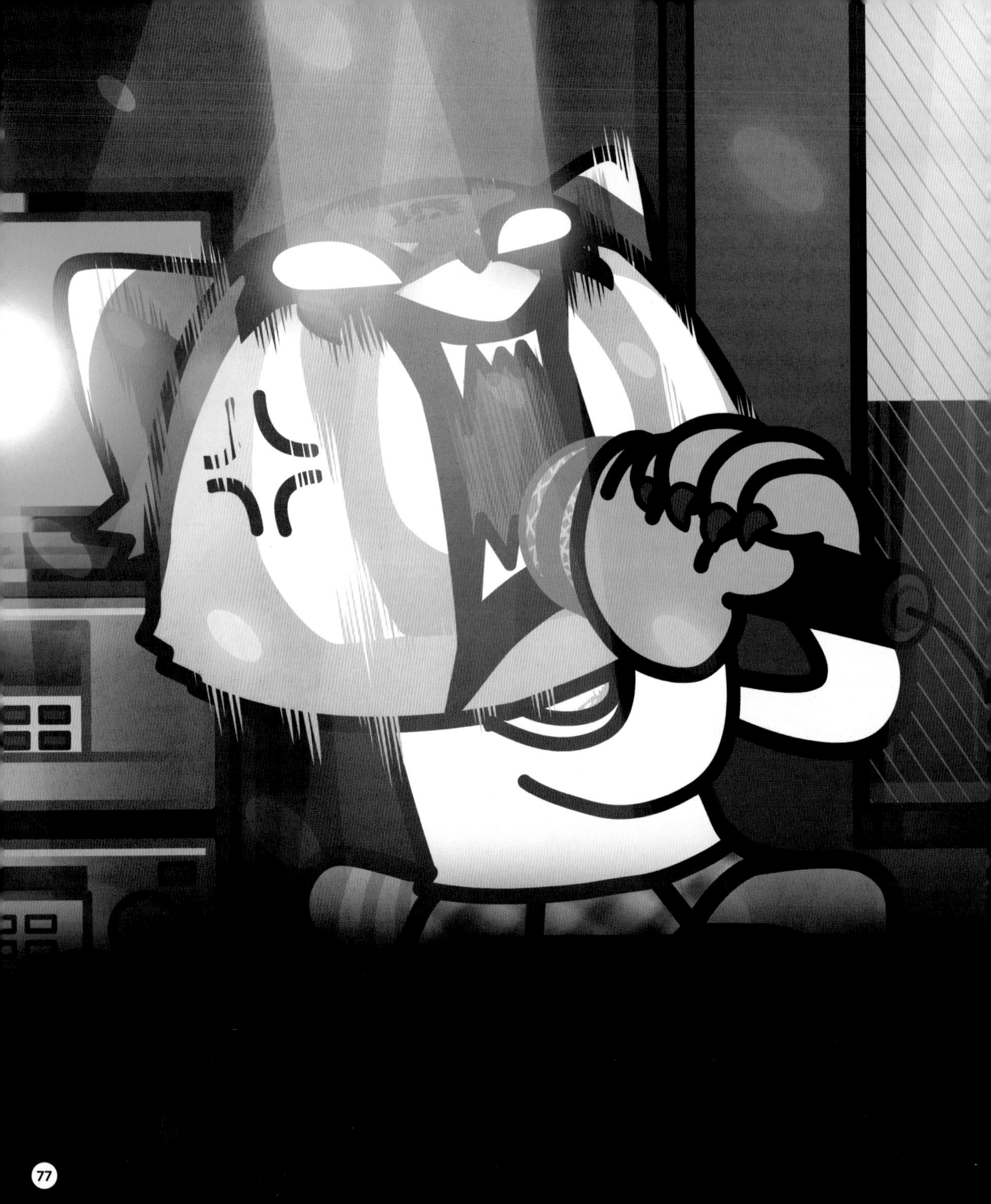

GO-TO KARAOKE SONGS

Here is a go-to list of favorite karaoke songs in no particular order.

AC/DC'S "WHOLE LOTTA ROSIE"
Not as widely sung as some of AC/DC's classics but you can't go wrong with this, baby. All attitude and screech, and a kicking bass line.

BLACK FLAG'S "RISE ABOVE"
Okay, this one veers a little more punk than metal but it'll get the entire bar yelling the chorus.

MOTÖRHEAD'S "ACE OF SPADES"
There's a reason this one's a classic.

METALLICA'S "ENTER SANDMAN"
A so-called wall of guitars—three guitar tracks of the same riff—gives this song its punch and when I'm done singing it, it's K.O.

BLACK SABBATH'S "PARANOID"
A signature song from one of the greatest.

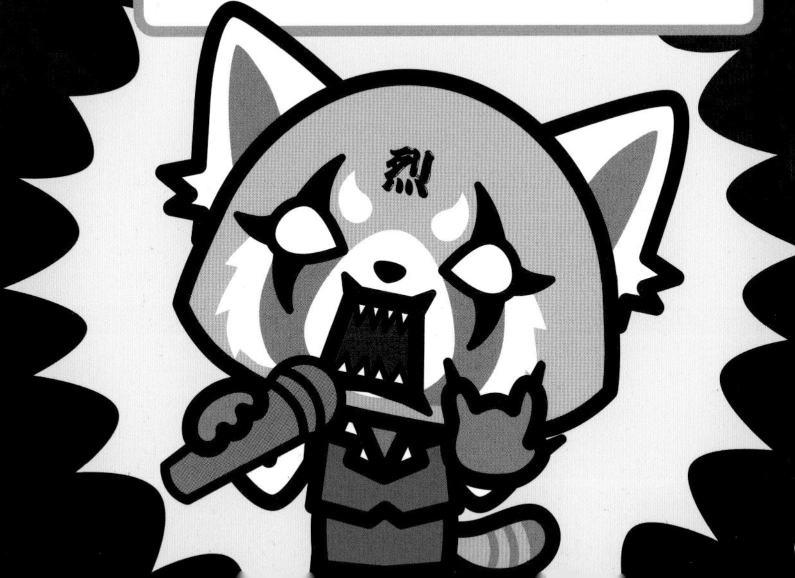
烈

BEST PLACES TO GET DRUNK

The mark of a good bar, in my opinion, is the ratio of annoying people to square footage. More doesn't necessarily mean merrier. Here's my ranking of the best places to drink away your work-related sorrows:

HONORABLE MENTION: MY HOME
The only reason my home isn't in first place ranking is because nine times out of ten it's just me, myself, and I, and I'm pretty sure you need another red panda in the room for it to be considered a real night out.

THIRD PLACE: THE DIVE BAR
The Dive Bar is King of low-brow. Nobody does two dollar beer better. If there are peanut shells on the floor, four people at the counter, and a dartboard in the back room, you've hit gold.

SECOND PLACE: THE AIRPORT BAR
No one can question a martini at 11 in the morning at an airport bar. It's five o'clock somewhere in the world, and you may have just de-planed from that very place. Also, it's a perfectly legitimate setting to order a cocktail with a mini umbrella in it and not feel like an idiot. After all, you're on vacation! Right?

FIRST PLACE: THE KARAOKE BAR
I don't need to explain this one.

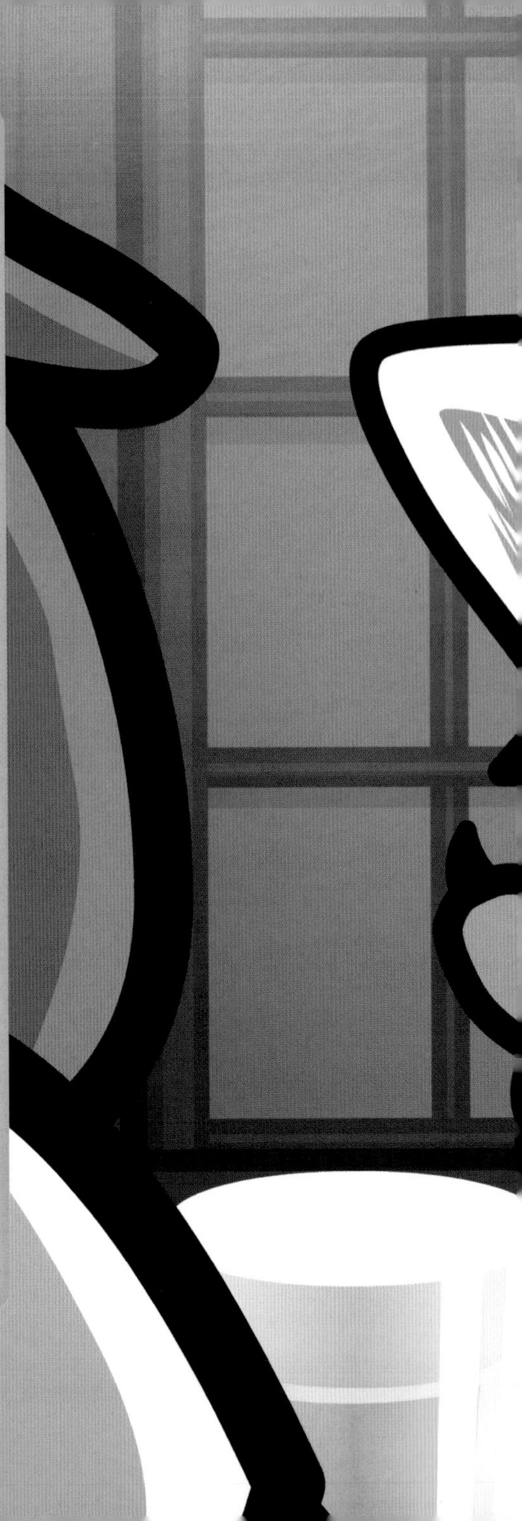

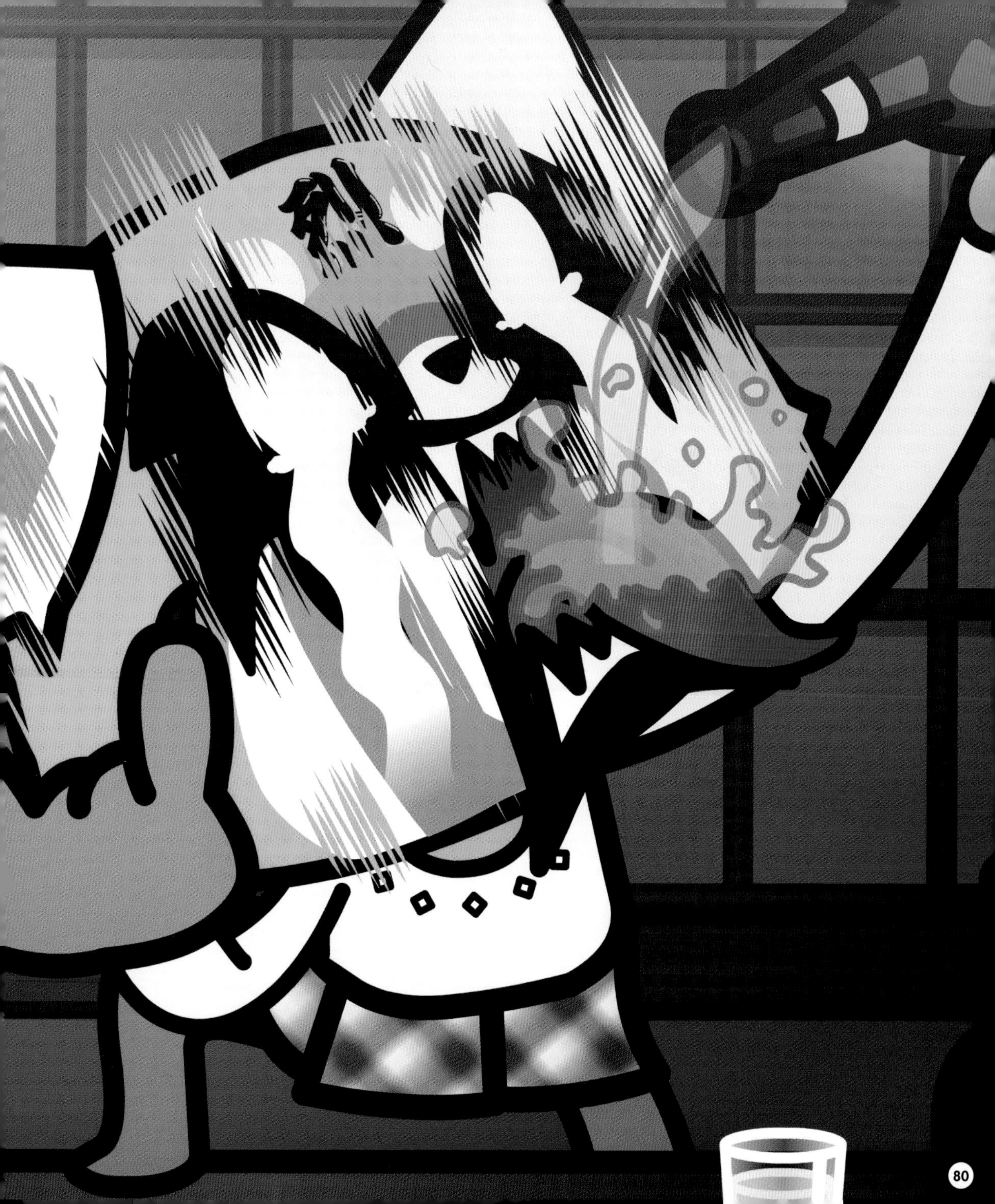
祭

THE DO'S AND DON'TS OF DRINKING WITH CO-WORKERS

DO ENJOY SOME DRINKS AND LAUGHS.

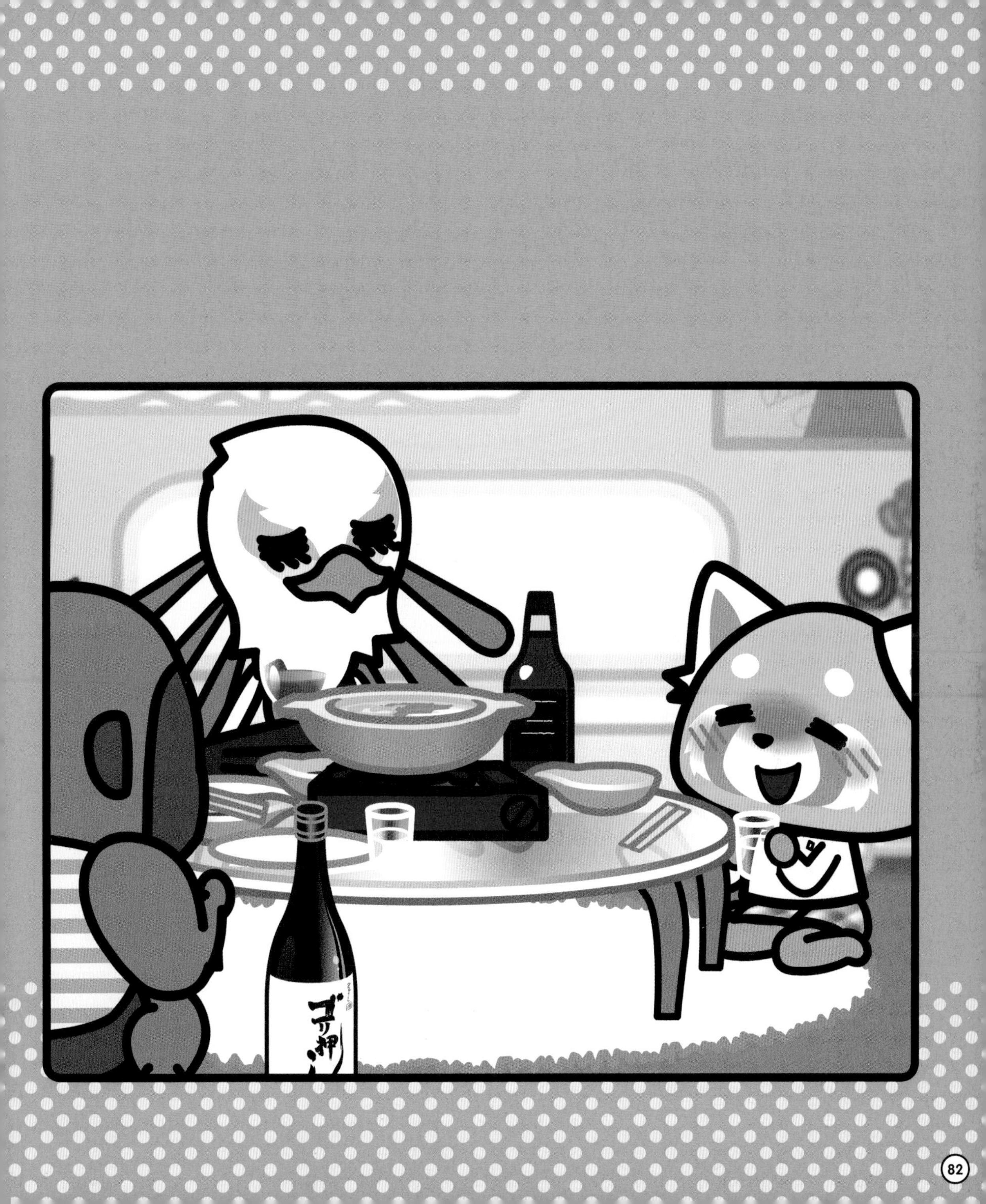
ゴリ押

THE DO'S AND DON'TS OF DRINKING WITH CO-WORKERS

DON'T GO TO A FORCED OUTING WITH SUPERIORS.

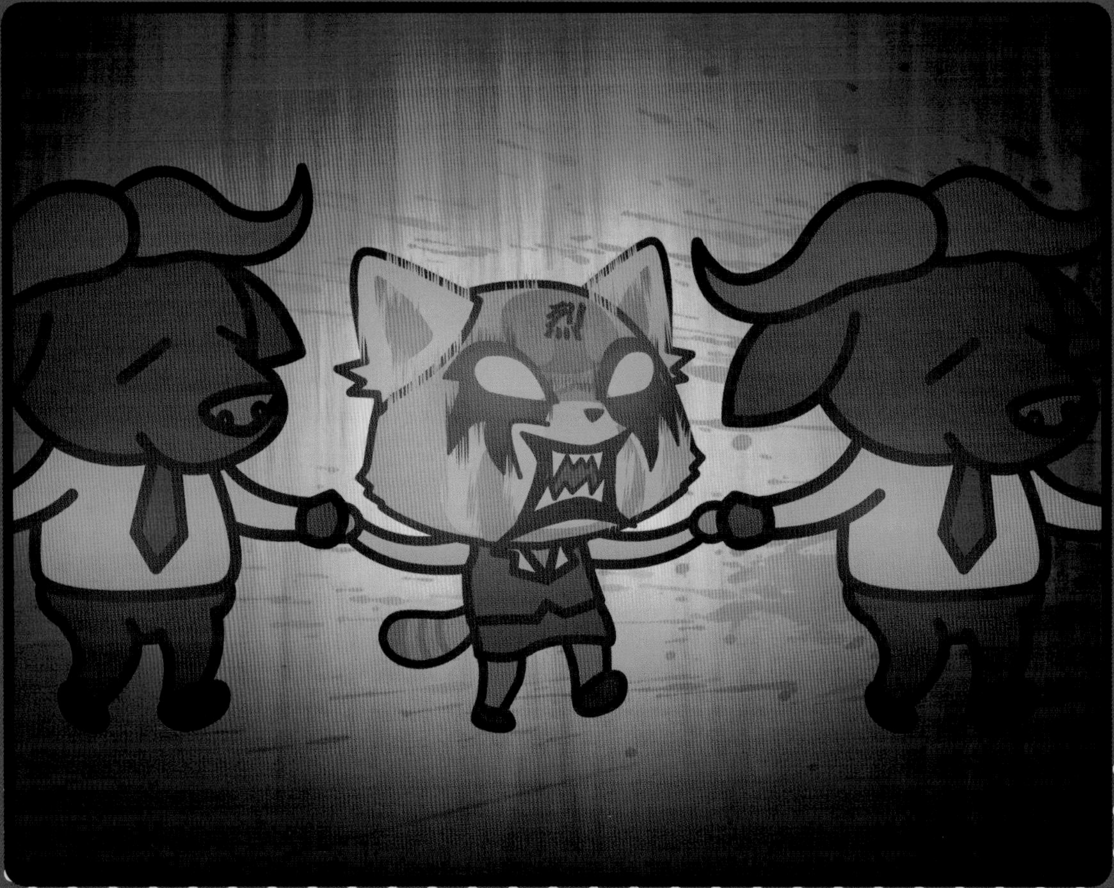

IT WILL BE DIFFICULT TO HIDE YOUR TRUE FEELINGS.

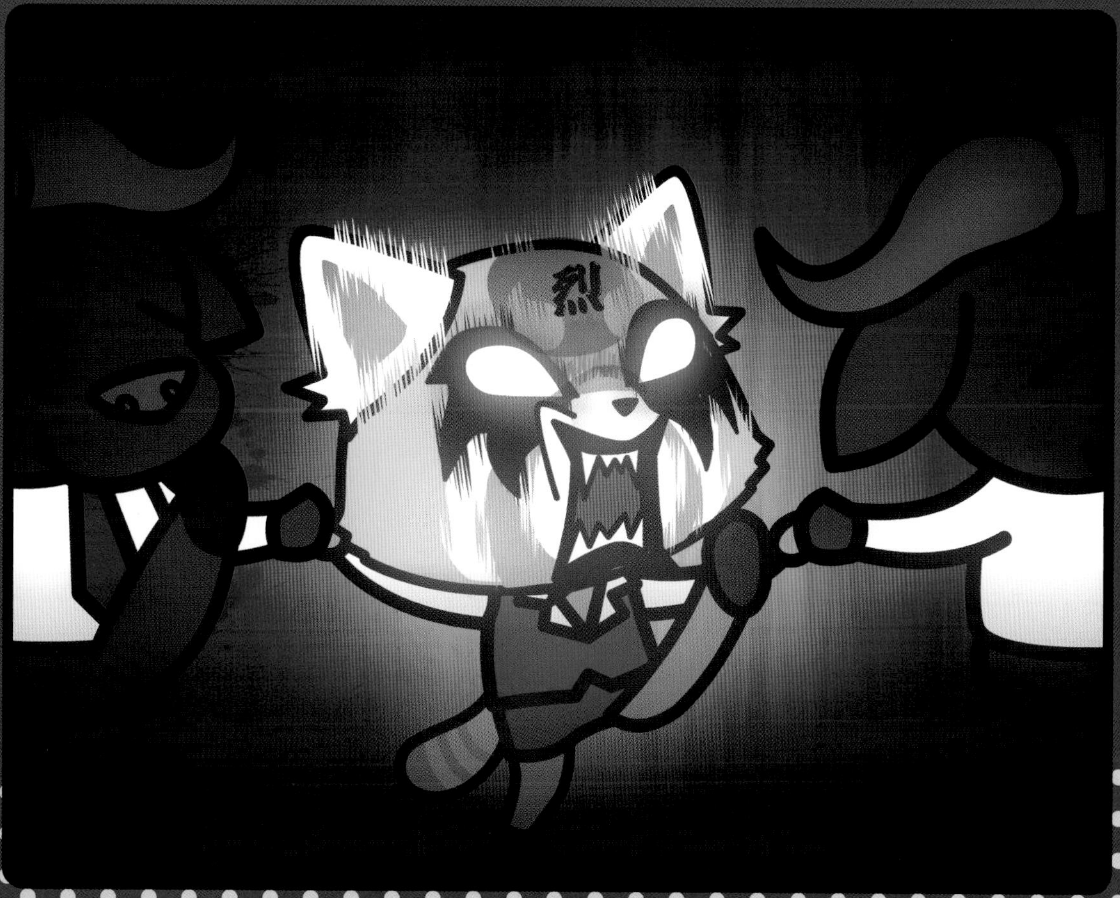
烈

SPLITTING THE BILL

While going out with colleagues can be fun, it can also be costly even when you least expect it. There's nothing worse than agreeing to go Dutch with your buddies when they decide to order enough food and alcohol to rival the weight of an African elephant. Always bring cash so that you can pay just your share of the tab—no one else's.

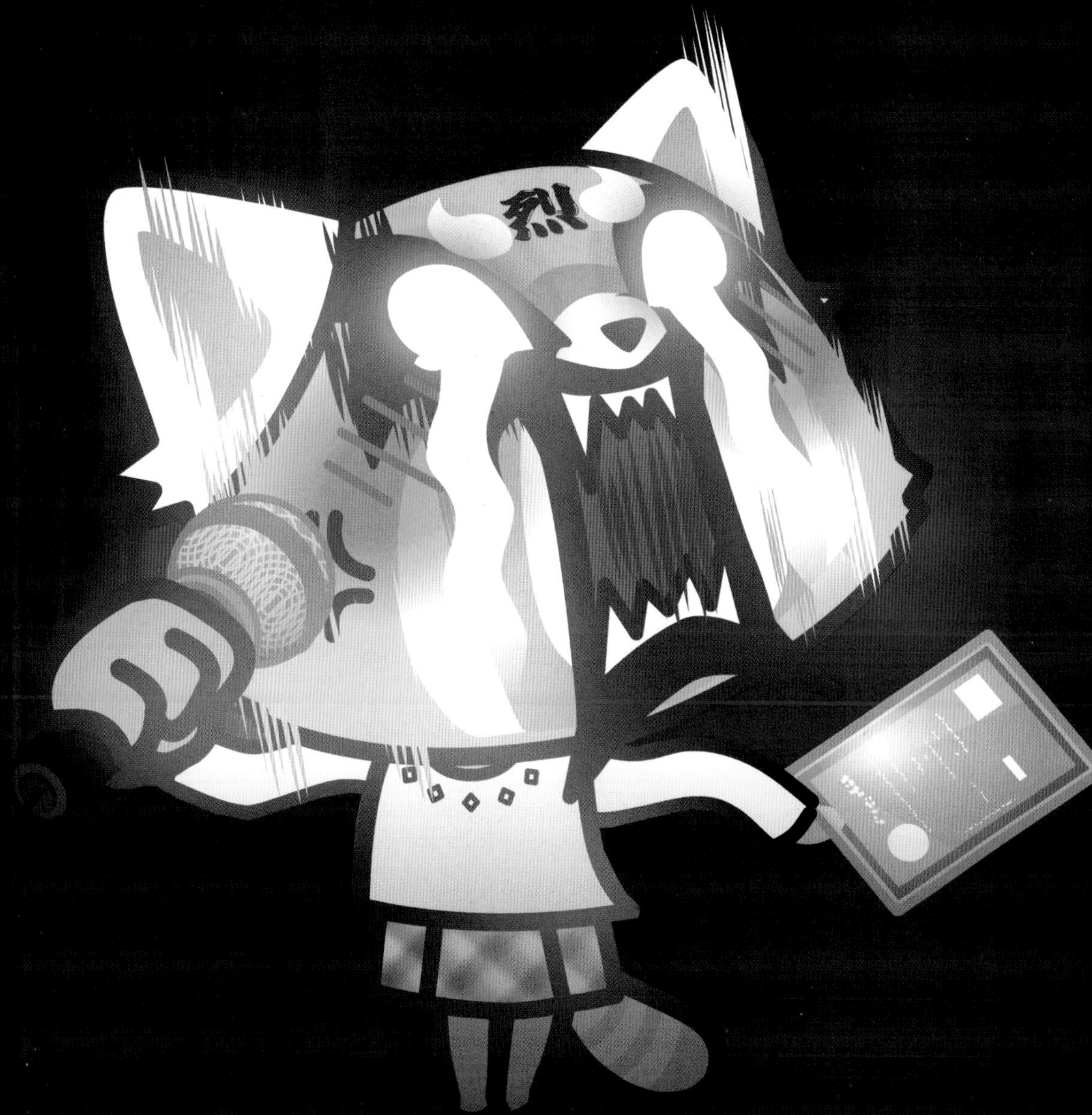
烈

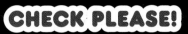

CHECK PLEASE!

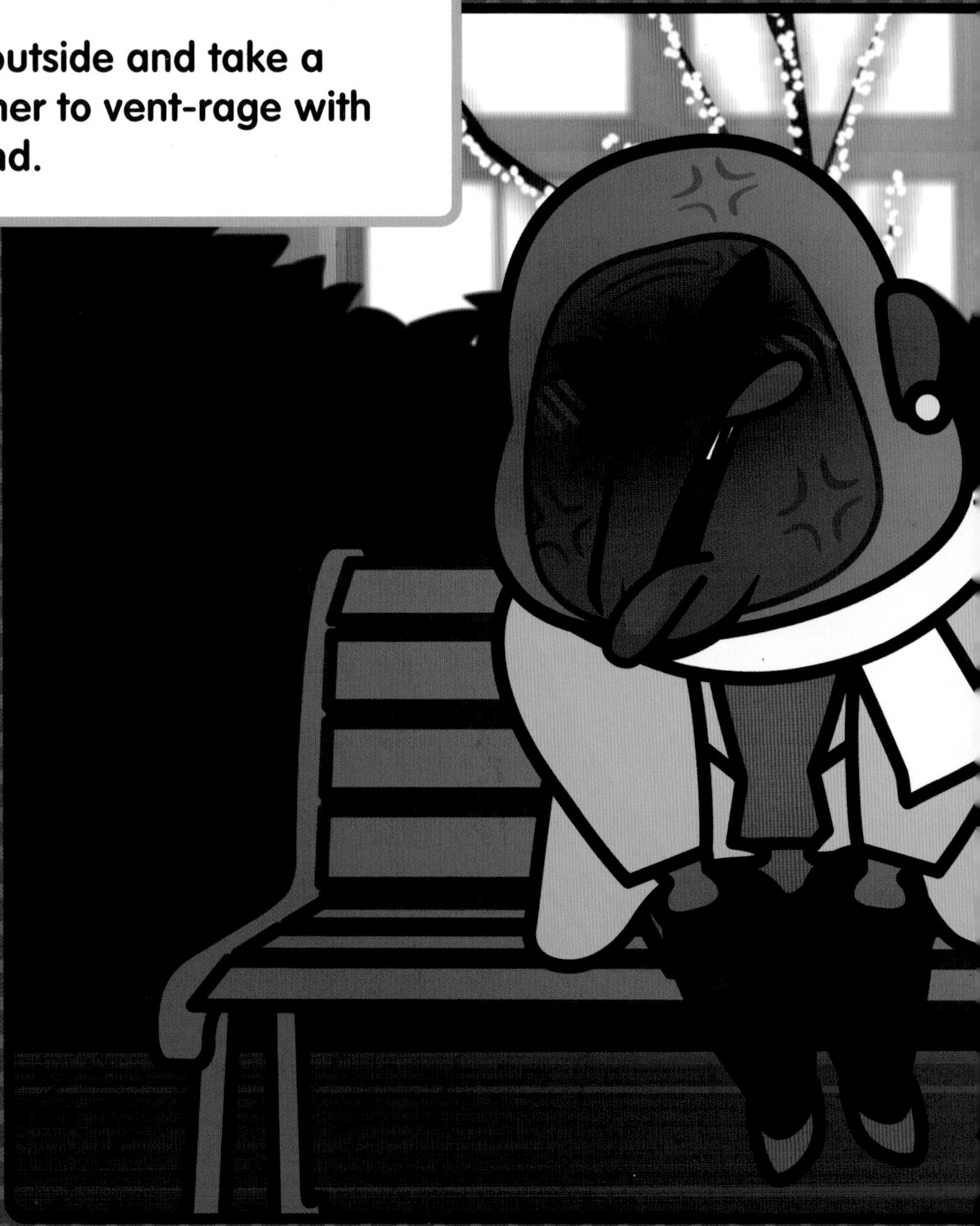

TIP

Step outside and take a breather to vent-rage with a friend.

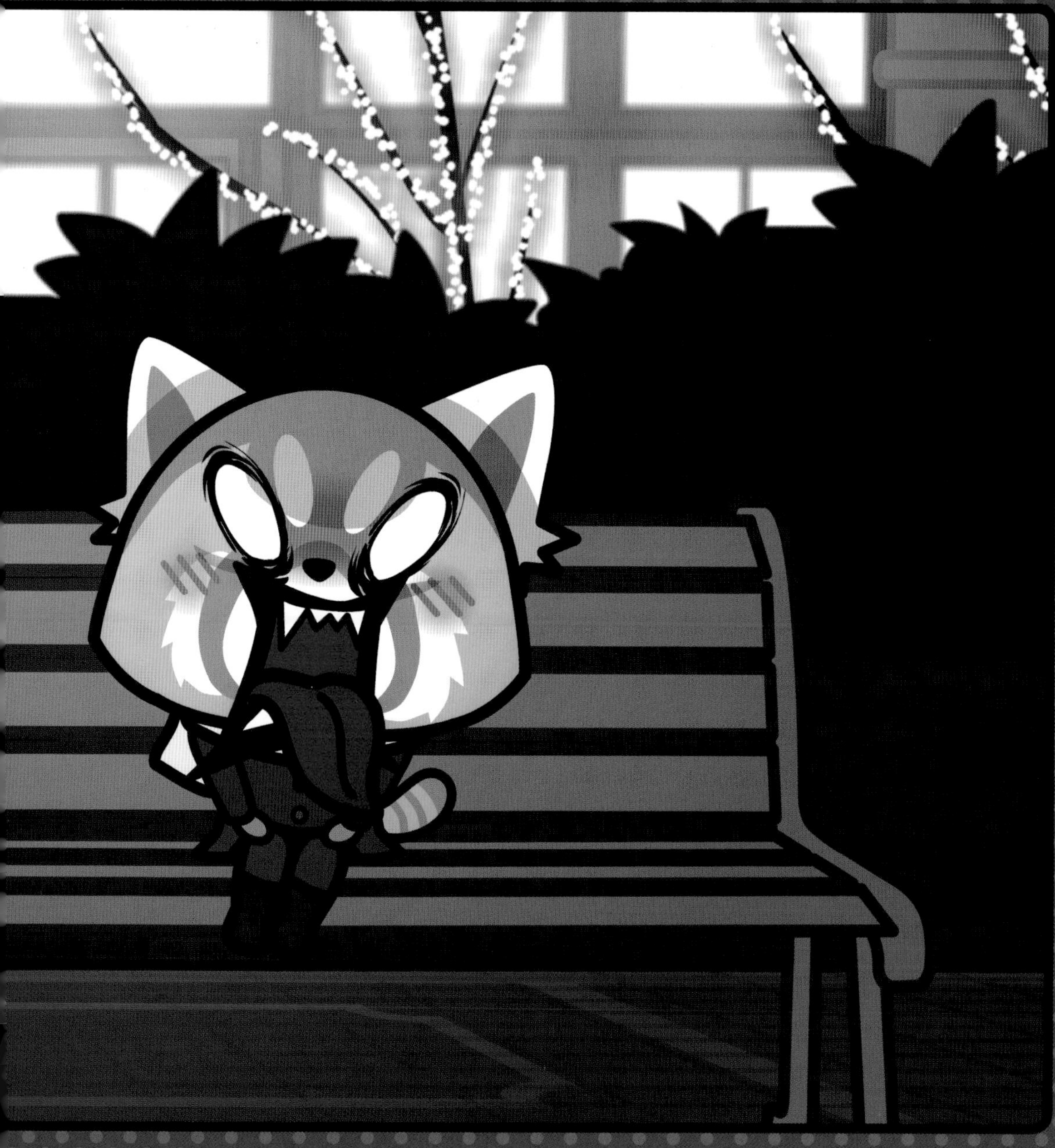

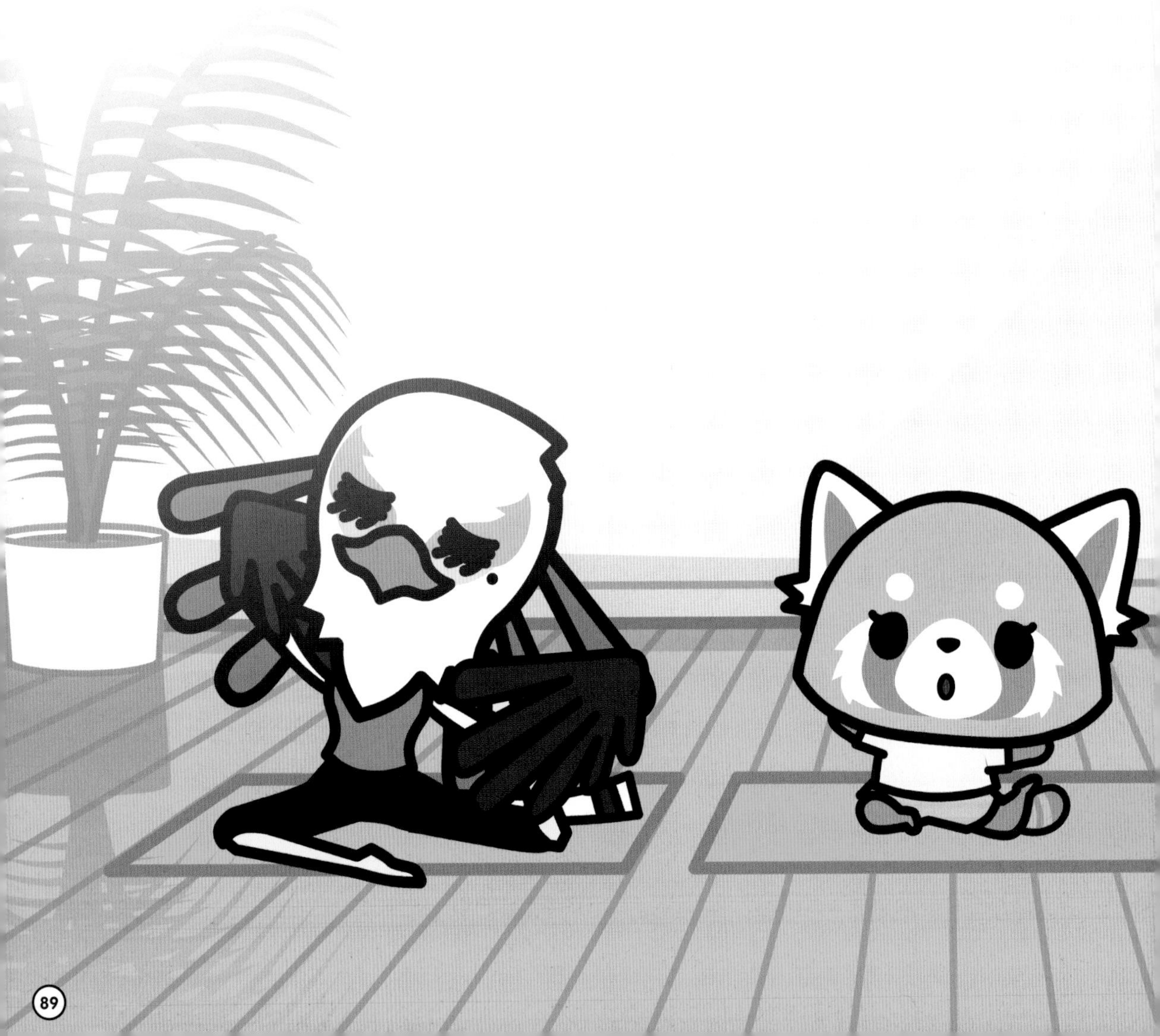

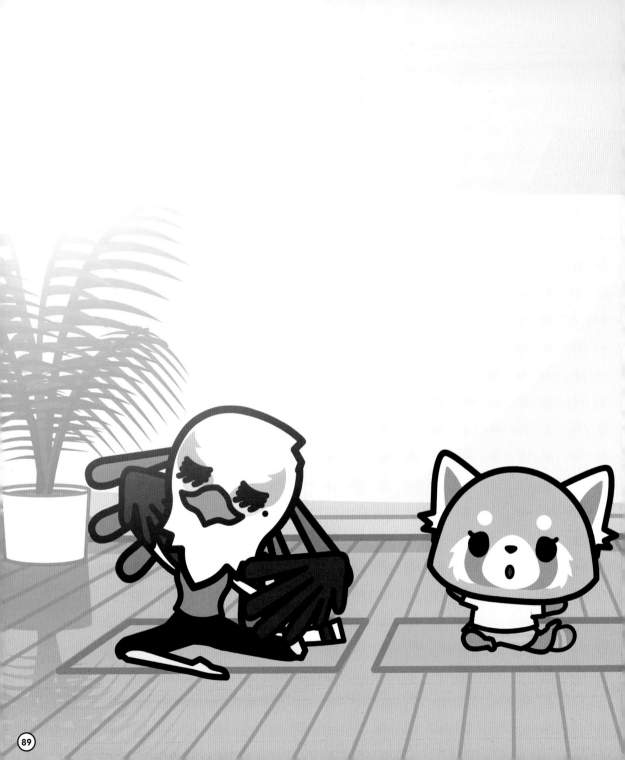

EPILOGUE: TOMORROW IS A NEW DAY!

When you think you can't take it anymore and your boss is breathing down your back, do not shrivel up and die. I know: easier said than done. I sometimes err on the side of shrinking flower but I've learned that you can't live your life hiding from the rage that burns inside. You can survive your days by clawing through the nine-to-five, year after year. Or you can thrive and live your life on your terms: loud and free. And if you, like me, are secretly a death metal thrasher inside, a beast waiting to be released, RAGE. And remember . . .

Tomorrow is a new day!

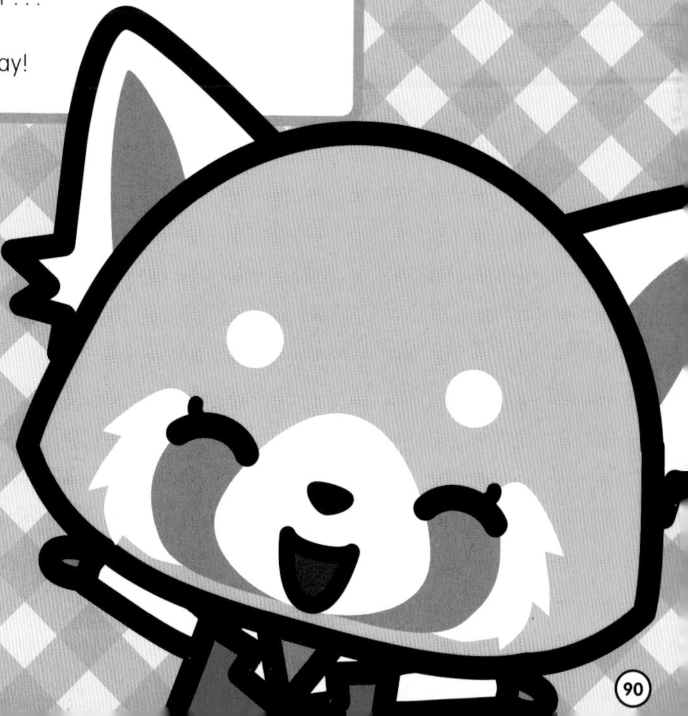

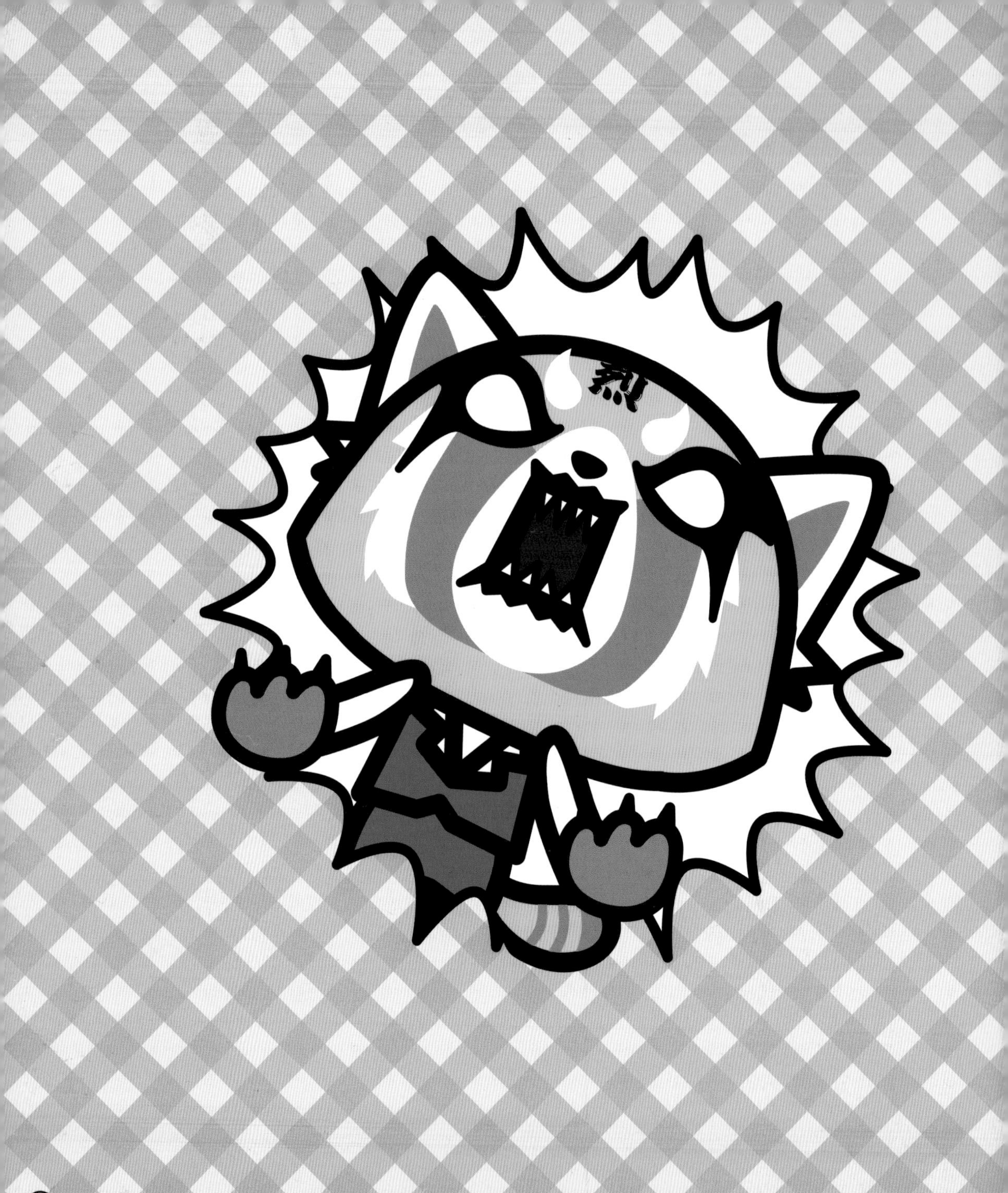
烈